D0623220

A TRIBUTE TO

KEITH MOON

(THERE IS NO SUBSTITUTE)

Compiled by Ian Snowball
& The Estate of Keith Moon

OMNIBUS PRESS
London • New York • Paris • Sydney • Copenhagen • Berlin • Madrid • Tokyo

Exclusive Distributors

Music Sales Limited
14/15 Berners Street, London, W1T 3LJ.

Music Sales Corporation
180 Madison Avenue, 24th Floor, New York, NY 10016, USA.

Music Sales Pty Ltd.
Australia and New Zealand
Level 4, 30-32 Carrington Street, Sydney, NSW 2000, Australia.

Printed in Croatia.

A catalogue record for this book
is available from the British Library.

Visit Omnibus Press on the web at
www.omnibuspress.com

KEITH MOON

(23.08.1946 – 07.09.1978)

THERE IS NO SUBSTITUTE

The words on Keith's plaque at Golders Green Crematorium

"Retarded artistically and idiotic in other respects."

Keith's school report from autumn 1959

"My mum often described Keith as being 'too big for this world,'
but while he was here he loved to get your attention! I feel he would
be glad of a book that keeps him alive in our hearts and minds.
Many thanks."

Amanda De Wolf, May 2015

NOTES & ACKNOWLEDGEMENTS
IAN SNOWBALL AUTHOR

Quite simply, I loved doing this book on Keith Moon, possibly more so than any other book that I have written or been involved with. Within weeks of coming up with the idea I had linked in with the Artist Legacy Group who look after Moon's estate and we had agreed to compile the book together. Things moved quickly and before I knew it I was sitting down on a warm summer's day with Kenney Jones on the terrace of his Hurtswood Polo Club at Ewhurst in Surrey. We spent over two hours chatting about Keith Moon, drumming, rock'n'roll and the sixties. We were both in our element. I appreciated the fact that Kenney didn't rush me or the interview. I truly believe he enjoyed sharing his thoughts and feelings about his old friend Keith Moon with me; but then why shouldn't he?

I spent the remainder of the summer of 2013 conducting interviews and piecing together my research. During that time I was fortunate to speak to some of the members of bands that have meant so much to me: Jim McCarty of The Yardbirds, Mick Avory of The Kinks, Don Powell of Slade, Rick Buckler of The Jam and Jack Bruce. Others to whom we owe a huge debt include Pete Townshend, Clem Burke, Mandy De Wolf, Paul De Wolf, Henry Root, Kelly Vallon and all the contributors in text and photographs, Marc Starke, Ashley and Scott Austin at ALG, Chris Charlesworth and the Omnibus team, my girlfriend Loz, my daughter Josie, Rick Buckler and David Lees at SME Protect Insurance Brokers.

I needed a foreword and only one name came to mind. I spoke to Clem Burke of Blondie whom everyone knows is a massive Moon fan, and he agreed to write it. And then one morning, after having met with Chris Charlesworth of Omnibus Press the previous day, I woke up to an email from Pete Townshend. His especially helpful PA Nicola Joss and I had been in contact and she helped to get Pete on board. (I also learned that Richard Barnes had a hand in it.) So then we had the introduction. As I read through Pete's words I honestly felt quite moved and so very pleased. It was then I realised that we had pulled it off. With a lot of help from a lot of Moon's friends, fans and peers, we had produced a fitting tribute book to Keith Moon. I spent that day grinning like a Cheshire cat.

Ian Snowball, May 2015

ASHLEY AUSTIN *THE ESTATE OF KEITH MOON*

Keith Moon had an insatiable appetite for life; tales of his excess and hilarious antics are now deeply woven into the fabric of rock'n'roll history.

However, the purpose of this book is not to reiterate the sensational stories that have been told countless times over the years, although the majority of them are true! When author Ian Snowball first reached out to us, we were delighted to find that he shared in our desire to explore the lighter side of the Moon–the man, the friend, the incendiary drummer.

Initially this book was going to contain reflections and accounts from those who knew him best; thankfully, the idea of allowing fans to submit their stories, photos and artwork was openly received by our publisher. What transpired from our call to action across Keith's social media profiles was a flood of personal memories and memorabilia from fans all over the world who have either spent time with or been inspired by him in one way or another.

Stories like these are the reason I do what I do. Keith Moon's contribution to pop culture is unparalleled, and what an honour it is to be entrusted to help preserve his legacy.

Thank you to all of Keith's peers, friends and fans who contributed their personal stories and photographs to this book. A very special thanks to Pete Townshend, Roger Daltrey, Bill Curbishley and Robert Rosenberg for their unyielding commitment to keeping Keith's memory alive, and for their continued support of the work we at Artist Legacy Group are doing on Keith's behalf.

Ashley Austin, May 2015

www.keithmoon.com

CLEM BURKE *BLONDIE*

It was the morning of 7 September 1978. I woke up in my hotel room in Rotterdam to prepare to leave for London and our shows with Blondie at the Hammersmith Odeon. I was in a great mood. I got in the lift and headed to the lobby where there in the hotel gift shop were all the UK daily papers with headlines like "Madman drummer of The Who, Keith Moon dead". I was devastated.

At the sound check the next day I asked my tech to get a hold of an axe and some petrol. It seemed no one was able to locate them. My intentions were obvious to everyone. At the end of the show that night I decided that since there was no axe or petrol I would sacrifice my kit by kicking it over, smashing it and throwing it into the audience after which I ran up to a mike and shouted "that was for Keith" as our crew jumped into the pit to try and get it back. I really didn't want them to do that.

In retrospect it may seem like a crazy thing to do but ever since I heard the first Who album Keith has been an inspiration to me; he is my muse. Keith Moon was not only an icon, he was an iconoclast. Keith played the drums like no one else. He was the perfect match to the fury of Townshend's guitar. The noise that they made together was like nothing that had come before in rock'n'roll.

The first Who album set the template for what was to follow. Keith's wild surf beat on the ironically titled 'The Ox' is pure energy and excitement! I recall as a youngster trying to play along to the ending of 'My Generation'; I'm still trying to get it right. Keith's playing is pure magic, a one man drum symphony–on 'A Quick One' it is so amazingly orchestrated as it goes through the various movements as the precursor to *Tommy*.

Keith was innovative, always playing the unexpected. There are so many great riffs and fills that are inspiring–just check out something like 'Young Man Blues' from *Live At Leeds*.

I'll never forget the scene in the film *The Kids Are Alright*–Keith's headphones gaffered to his head playing along to the synthesizer sequence. Talk about being ahead of his time, that's what most modern drummers are doing today in concert!

Although Keith was a massive inspiration to me, he also made me realise the possibility of tragedy in the rock'n'roll lifestyle. Keith's early passing serves as a life lesson to all in the game. So let's hear it for the one and only great Keith Moon!

Clem Burke 2015

Left: Not for the first time and certainly not the last, Keith demolishes his Pictures of Lily kit on stage.

INTRODUCTION
PETE TOWNSHEND

An image of Keith comes to mind of the way he was often deeply reflective. Sitting opposite him at a table one would watch him take a wooden toothpick and pick absentmindedly and without reason at his front teeth. He always kept his mouth closed when he did this. His almost black eyes would look into the distance, and his mouth would pout, and then in one of his most characteristic mannerisms he would swing the pout to one side as though he was using it as rudder. It would be a signal. The faraway look would disappear and he would return to the room and in the early days come up with some joke or secondhand story that he thought would amuse. In later days it might be the signal for him to demand money, without saying why, and generally I gave it to him.

In the very early days I suppose I was a little enamoured of him. Not sexually; he was a rather lumpy fellow physically, and any homoerotic feelings I had were towards the more conventional handsome men of the day like Chris Stamp, our manager, or – as is now well known – Mick Jagger. But he was like Kit Lambert who was equally eccentric and prone to move in an instant from reverie to outbursts of humour, and was easy to love. Despite the liberalisation of the sixties it was rare to hear men speak to each other of love at any level. Today, men are tough enough and easy enough to tell each other if there is a bond.

I think it's fairly safe to say that Keith was the first man to ever say he loved me, in his last days

sadly, but I believed him, and I think he might have been the first man I was able to sincerely tell I felt the same way.

And so when I think of him it is not as a drummer, or a crazy man who indulged in stunts, but as someone whom I admired, whom I enjoyed being with, whose small foibles all seemed attractive and engaging to me. He was, above all things, very funny, with a great memory for gags and finding ways to bring them into everyday conversation. But he was also earnest and imaginative, and it was very rare that I bored of being in his company.

Of course his drumming style was important to the way I wrote songs. I produced demos of most of my songs and as soon as I had the space I started to play the drums myself on those demos on a small kit Keith gave me (that I still own). The drumming style I favoured was rather more early R&B flavoured: like the very simple patterns played

Left: The Who at Shepperton Studios 1976. Right: Pete in his home studio in 1973 with the drum kit given to him by Keith.

on Jimmy Reed or Booker T recordings. Tamla Motown drummers were experimenting with more complex rhythms like that used on 'Dance To Keep From Crying' and 'Reach Out' but Keith's style was derived from jazz I think – and yet he found it very hard to swing in a jazz manner. His playing was always on the beat, driving, moving forward. Charlie Watts always swung, and was quite the opposite in that he found it hard to play on the beat and drive, but their respective methods were both inspired by jazz. Keith decorated as he played, he punctuated and marked music events like an orchestral drummer. Some of his fills were incredibly complex, but undisciplined, and they didn't always come off. But his playing was also humorous. And so when I was writing I tried on my demos to indicate what Keith might like to play to suit the song, and he never took umbrage at what I had played, or mentioned that I was not particularly good at drumming. He seemed to appreciate the thought and effort I put into the demos.

The high period of Keith's drumming was of course *Quadrophenia*, and my drumming on the demos was probably at its best around this time. Later (with *Who By Numbers* and *Who Are You*) I became very conventional and actually started to play like a session player, and the link between my song writing demos and Keith's playing was broken.

I think the word I would use to describe Keith's style of drumming is 'free' rather than 'anarchic'. He knew no boundaries.

It does surprise me that there is still so much interest in Keith as a drummer because very few of our musician-peers seemed to appreciate Keith's style. Ronnie Lane – for example – adored Keith but I think he thought his drumming had a deleterious effect on my songs. But Buddy Rich liked Keith's playing, and so did other jazz drummers I met, like Tony Williams. These two guys alone must provide a testament, really the top two jazz drummers of

Right: Free rather than anarchic, Keith knew no boundaries.

Pete with John Entwistle and Keith on Beat Club, German TV 1966.

the sixties. The jazz-trained Charlie Watts also loved Keith's fluid style. I think Keith's biggest fan was John Bonham who always watched Keith intently when he could (sitting in for the entire recording of 'Won't Get Fooled Again').

The loon stuff was a big part of Keith's world. His stunts created a constant flow of PR for The Who, otherwise we might have discouraged him. They were mostly very funny, but not always. I often felt sorry for Keith when he was in his most ostentatious mode, off stage. It was almost as though he felt his stage work was not enough; that he had to keep performing.

Pete Townshend

KEITH MOON
ANYWAY, ANYHOW, ANYWHERE

In 2011, 33 years after his death, Keith Moon was voted the second greatest drummer in history in a readers' poll conducted by *Rolling Stone* magazine. Thankfully there have been several books about him, including two, *Full Moon* and *Keith Moon – A Personal Portrait*, by his personal assistant Peter 'Dougal' Butler; *Dear Boy*, a 600 plus page definitive biography, by Tony Fletcher; and *Instant Party* by Alan Clayson. There are also sterling books on The Who, including *The Who: Maximum R&B* by Richard Barnes, *Before I Get Old* by Dave Marsh and *Pretend You're In A War* by Mark Blake, not to mention rigorously researched chronologies like *Anyway Anyhow Anywhere* by Andy Neill and Matt Kent, and *The Who Concert File* by Joe McMichael and 'Irish' Jack Lyons. All these books contribute to a better understanding of Keith Moon as a man and as the drummer in The Who, and it is surely instructive that at least one of them, *Dear Boy,* published in 1998, has now sold well over 100,000 copies worldwide.

The wild and outrageous stories have therefore been well-told and well-read, but this book has deliberately swerved this aspect of the Moon legend so as not to revisit old ground. During Keith's life he was here, there and everywhere, fooling about in the world's greatest clubs and playing drums with one of the world's greatest rock bands on the world's greatest stages. Keith knew everyone and everyone wanted to know him, and not just because he would buy everyone a drink. Keith hung out with a who's who of rock'n'roll from the early days of The Who right to the end of his life – Paul McCartney was his dinner companion on the night he died.

Keith could be seen playing at all the cool and legendary venues of the sixties, like the Marquee,

and before that, when they were The High Numbers, at the Scene Club, one of London's earliest Mod clubs. Although not every Mod's 'cup of tea' 'top' Mods preferred the original versions of R&B songs covered by them – by the time their debut LP *My Generation* was released in 1965 The Who had amassed a loyal following that embraced them with arms wide open. The Who's fan base continued to swell and grow throughout the remainder of the sixties and long into the seventies right up until 7 September 1978. Then The Who, as the world had known them, ceased to be.

Keith's first group was Mark Twain & The Strangers and at 16 he joined The Beachcombers, a semi-pro outfit that worked the West London circuit. He was far younger than the rest of the group, not that this bothered him. He was more than happy to drum with a working band and even play Shadows' instrumentals. Early drum lessons with Carlo Little set him on his way and from the day of his Beachcombers audition his personality and skill on the kit shone brightly. By the time he left The Beachcombers to join The Who he was well on his way to becoming a star drummer.

The Who was the band that Keith was born to play for. Briefly changing their name to The High Numbers, they released 'I'm The Face', a shameless attempt at appealing to Mods, the cool kids, who had adopted them as fellow travellers. Then managed by uber-Mod Pete Meaden, the connection served them well and the four members of The Who – guitarist Pete Townshend, singer Roger Daltrey, bassist John Entwistle and drummer boy Keith – allowed themselves to be swept along in the Mod tide that suited them as individuals and chimed with their music. Keith threw himself into

Left: Keith with one of his first Premier kits with two bass drums at the Marquee Club, London, 2 March 1967 being filmed for Beat Club aus London, *a TV special for NDR, Germany.*

the lifestyle, playing hard on stage and off, an early convert to pills that would keep him awake all night and others that finally knocked him out.

For those outside of West London, The Who exploded into our consciousness in 1965, the year of 'I Can't Explain', of *Ready Steady Go!*, of 'Anyway Anyhow Anywhere' and of 'My Generation'. It was also the year when Keith began his campaign of blowing up toilets, initially stuffing Cherry Bombs down loos before progressing to fireworks and then dynamite. A year later, in Berlin, he decided that smashing up hotel rooms was the best way to signal his disaffection for tardy room service, and this would become a constant feature in his life, a continual source of material for journalists to document. But while these antics earned Keith the title 'Moon The Loon', there was much more to Keith than all that. On the pages that follow we celebrate the life of Keith Moon the drummer, the musician and the man, and not just a man who smashed up hotels or drove his Rolls Royce into a swimming pool – well, a pond, as it happens.

The drums at the end of 'Love Reign O'er Me', the song that closes *Quadrophenia*, pound with such conviction that you can almost imagine Keith grinning as he bangs away, leaning into his kit, his arms a blur as they spin across the skins and, at the climax, demolishing his kit in the studio. This extraordinary performance was among Keith's last great contributions to The Who's catalogue, joining a couple of other tracks that closed Who albums – 'Rael' and 'Won't Get Fooled Again' – as moments of transcendence that other drummers continue to revere. Many of them offer their tributes in these pages.

Keith gave his final interview to presenter David Hartman on the *Good Morning America* TV show on 7 August 1978. Keith sat relaxed on the sofa on Pete's right, wearing a bright red shirt with gold chains around his neck, a black jacket and flared white trousers, punk's sharper look having evidently failed to jettison Keith's penchant for the flamboyant clothes worn earlier in the decade. Asked when he is in control of his own life, Keith replies, "Oh yeah, certain days". It's tinged with humour and Keith follows up by joking about an altercation with Roger and John back at the hotel, which is why they were not present on the show. It's a fabrication – Roger and John were back in England – but as ever it's Keith playing with the interviewer. Pete intervenes by informing Hartman that "One thing you can guarantee is that he (Keith) is never serious."

The interview continues with Pete mostly fielding questions about The Who and how they fit in their personal and social lives around the band and being on the road. When Keith is asked if he'd rather be on the road than at home, he replies, "Yes I would. I enjoy being on the road very much." Unfortunately Pete and Roger didn't agree, at least at that point in their lives.

The interviewer then asks "When you're all in your fifties do you think you'll still be together?" to which Keith responds with, "Yeah, in some form or another", and then goes on to talk about The Who's current and forthcoming projects in music and film. "We won't be The Who on the road, but we'll be producing and creating," he adds.

Keith Moon died exactly one month later in his bed at 9 Curzon Place, the same apartment and bedroom where Mama Cass died four years earlier. He is still mourned by fans worldwide.

Right: Not To Be Taken Away. Keith with Pete, John and Roger at Shepperton Studios, Friday 26 May 1978.

KENNEY JONES   DON POWELL   MICK AVORY
JACK BRUCE   CARL PALMER   NEAL SMITH   DENNIS
'MACHINE GUN' THOMPSON   RICHARD BARNES
RICK BUCKLER   STEVE WHITE TODD   SUCHERMAN
PETER 'DOUGAL' BUTLER   'LEGS' LARRY SMITH
JOHN MAHER   JOHN MEARS   JOHN SCHOLLAR
TONY BARBADOS   CHARLIE MOON FOX
CHRIS CHARLESWORTH   DARRIN MOONEY
PHIL GOULD   IAN McNABB   JIM McCARTY   JOHN
COGHLAN   MAX WEINBERG   DEBBI PETERSON
NEVILLE CHESTERS   EDDIE PHILLIPS   AL MURRAY
TONY FLETCHER   JOHN PEUTHERER   DENISE
DUFORT   RICHARD COLE   RICHARD EVANS
RICHARD NEWMAN GEORGIANA STEELE-WALLER
JOHNNY ECHOLS   KIERON MAUGHAN   BRAD
ROGERS   MATTHEW BRAIM   BINKY PHILIPS
MATTHEW J BRADLEY   SCOTT 'PINETOP'
PETERSON   LAWRENCE STREMBA   KAITLIN
HAWK   EDDIE TUDURI   RAY DREDGE
CRAIG GILL   PAUL KEMP   DAN MAIDEN-WOOD
MATHEW PRIEST   SAM KESTEVEN   CHRIS
PUNTER   JOE GIORGIANNI   MISS JOSH
EMMETT   LORENA PEREIRA   HARRISON
KRAMER   JONATHAN LOUIS   JOE GORELICK
NATHAN HERSHFELD   GEORGE MANNEY
SHAWN LACKIE   RENEE KATHLEEN   JAY
MAHONEY   JOE RAMERSA   MICHAEL
BUTLER   SUE GILLIES   JANE QUINN

CAN YOU SEE THE REAL ME?

KENNEY JONES

SMALL FACES / THE FACES / THE WHO

"What's the first thing that comes to mind when I think of Keith Moon?" The first thing is I wish he was still here. I wish I could pick up the phone and arrange to meet up with him this afternoon. Keith was a very close friend and he is very much missed.

"I saw Keith at the Buddy Holly film party and that night he was still fun to be around. We had this relationship where he would never take the piss out of me. We could sit and talk without him feeling like he needed to be on show. I mean I saw plenty of Keith Moon 'the showman' too; you couldn't stop him, it was in his genes. We talked frankly about things and about both of our new projects, I was just starting up a new band with a couple of American guys and he was very interested. We were both talking very enthusiastically about what each other was doing. I remember it being a very positive conversation. Then we went off to watch the film and then I saw him again in the foyer on the way out.

"The next morning I got up and turned on the TV and the news about Keith's death was all over it. 'Keith Moon found dead from a drug overdose'. I didn't believe it, I couldn't believe it. I thought it was another one of Keith's hoaxes. I just kept telling myself that it couldn't be real. I mean I had only been with him a few hours earlier. But sure enough as the day developed, sure enough the news of Keith's death was true.

"From what I could gather he had taken one of the pills that he was on, gone to sleep, then woke

The Buddy Holly film party, Peppermint Park, London, 6 September 1978; David Frost, Kenney Jones, Annette Walter-Lax and Keith.

up and thinking it was the morning, he took another one and this was dangerous to the extent that it slowed his heart down, until it stopped. So in the end it was an indirect overdose of drugs that contributed to Keith's death. Now they may have found some other bits and bobs in his body, but I must say he really was trying to keep himself together. And what I like to think is that he would have been on the road to recovery. I suspect he would have had a couple of relapses, because that was Keith, but I think he would have kept going in the right direction and made larger leaps as time passed. That's what I like to believe.

"When The Small Faces had our first hit record, The Who had only had theirs a few months earlier. The press at the time thought it would be good if they made The Small Faces and The Who out to be rival bands. I think they based this on the fact that we were both from opposite ends of London. The funny thing was that because we were from the East End we thought anything outside of the East End was posh. So we thought The Who were posh. Little did we know what Shepherd's Bush was really like.

"The press tried to paint some kind of picture about how both bands hated each other's guts but of course it wasn't true. In actual fact it was the complete opposite and when both bands did meet up we all got on like a house on fire. Such was our relationship that we went touring around England, Europe and Australia together and that was a real laugh.

"We got on in lots of different ways, so much so that Pete Townshend used to ring me up and ask me to play drums on some of his demos. At the time he was living in a little house in Twickenham and he had his equipment set up in a small room upstairs. There was a fireplace in the room and I used to put the bass drum in the fireplace so that the sound would go up the chimney and help keep the boom noise down a bit.

"On the whole both members of both bands did quite a lot together. I even used to do some of The Who's sound checks for them when Keith wasn't there, for some reason or another. I used to sit behind Keith's kit and think 'My god, what are all these drums for?'

"I became very familiar with Keith's drum kits over the years. It was unusual because he never really used a hi-hat. It was strange to see another drummer without hi-hats. I mean hi-hats are quite an integral part of a drum kit in helping to keep a beat. I think a hi-hat restricted Keith. I think he felt trapped by it and if it was included in the set-up he would have to play a certain way, but if it wasn't there he could be more expressive. When I played in The Who I did try and come off the hi-hats and try to add more cymbal work.

"Later on, once I got to play with The Who and I was learning the songs I tried to put myself in Keith's shoes; but it was just impossible. He would put drum fills in places where they shouldn't go. The funny thing is I can probably play those Who songs better now than when I did back then.

AUSTRALIA

WHO   SMALL FACES

'Ban these scruffy urchins once and for all...'

"Pete Townshend sums Keith up the best way when he says that Keith had a built-in metronome and although he could go in and out of the song or the timing, Keith would still be there playing in time and still come in at the right moments.

"When you watched Keith, you couldn't help but be mesmerised by him. Sometimes I used to sit right behind or beside him on the stage and watch him. He would do the same with me. We appreciated each other in that way. But many times I would see him do something and think, 'How did he do that?'

The songs by The Who had a lot to do with the way Keith played. I mean if you put a Rolling Stones song on you automatically fall into a typical swingy 4/4 blues rock rhythm, but there are many different ways of playing 4/4s. There are all sorts of twists and skips that can be added. When you watch Charlie [Watts] you can see he does some unusual things with his right hand, which allows his left to deliver the beat with something different. I think it's a habit that he has developed that has worked for him.

"In Keith's early days he listened to drummers like Gene Krupa and I think he was trying to discover his own style, he was looking for his own personality and then he wanted to put his stamp on it. We were the first rock drummers but what we did was to play our interpretation of what we had been listening to.

"People often say that Keith watched and followed Townshend; I totally understand this, I did too. As the drummer you sit in the driving seat and it's a very special seat. When I played in The Who it was like sitting in between two lead guitarists. John Entwistle was such a fast precision bass player that my kick drum foot got incredibly quick. I learned a lot playing along to John's bass playing. I had a pretty good pedal foot before The Who but with The Who I learned to put bass drum patterns in different places.

"The idea that the drummer and the bass player must always work together I heard a lot when I started with The Small Faces, but even then I would say no. Instead I listened to Steve Marriott. It worked because Ronnie Lane and me clicked straight away anyway. Ronnie was a great bass player and very melodic. When we first met he was playing lead guitar. Then one day he said to me, 'I don't wanna do this anymore, I wanna play bass'. His lead guitar style then came out in his bass playing.

"So with Townshend you never know where the song is going to go. He was very much the band leader, he was like an orchestra conductor and you had to watch him. No Who songs live were ever played exactly the same way. The arrangements were more or less as they were but when we played we would go anywhere inside of that and that was fucking fantastic. I loved it; that suited me, it was what I had done with The Small Faces. Having Pete Townshend on one side and John Entwistle on the other was quite an experience. You couldn't help but be influenced and spellbound by the two of them and that would have affected Keith too. Playing with The Who was a treasured moment for me; the communication between us was very telepathic. I played with Roger and Pete recently and John was very much missed.

"Keith was very deliberate with his style of drumming. He was having fun with the serious side of his drumming. Keith was always on the edge but he had the serious side that would go and record. It's these two sides that made us laugh and love him to bits.

"I don't know if Keith thought that he was one of the great drummers but I feel that he was proud to be the drummer that he was. He was so great to watch and he did get a lot of praise and he was so completely different to anyone else on the scene. I have always said, 'There is only one drummer that's right for The Who and that is Keith Moon', and for me that is as simple as it gets."

Right: Keith at the Pavilion, Bath, Monday 10 October 1966.

DON POWELL

SLADE

"I think Keith's musicianship doesn't get the recognition that it deserves. I think people focused on Pete Townshend or Roger Daltrey and missed how much of an integral part Keith was. As a drummer myself, I listen to those early records and I don't know how he did some of those drum fills. I wonder if Keith realised himself.

"Keith was one of the pioneers of that rock style of drumming. I mean if you listen to the drumming on a song like 'Substitute', it's phenomenal. And even today I've never heard anybody come anywhere near Keith's style of drumming. I think even John Bonham would agree with me on that

one. What Keith did was play off the wall. He just didn't play anything that was normal. I think Keith played very instinctive and very much from the heart. That's the way his drumming came out of him.

"There were many early Slade songs that I played on, such as 'Cum On Feel The Noize', where I played the whole song just on the snare drum. That started because we used to go into a small rehearsal room and because the room was so tiny all you could hear were the drums; so I switched to just using the snare to try and keep the noise down. Jim Lea said 'Keep it', and that's what I did. At the time, to only use the snare was not the norm but Keith did lots of unusual things. He hardly ever used a hi-hat; instead he played what would normally be done on the hi-hats on the toms or the cymbals. He loved to smash the crash cymbal. I think Keith did open up a doorway for rock drummers.

"There were just no rules for Keith. Most drummers stick to rules the way they use the hi-hats and snares and so on to try to keep a steady thing going, but Keith, he just went for it, lock, stock and barrel. Come to think about it, I have never played along to a Who song, I don't think I actually could.

"For sure the songs that Pete [Townshend] wrote loaned themselves to Keith's style. In a way it was as if Keith played one of the lead instruments. When you hear a Who record Keith's drumming is one of the first things that hit you. It totally worked for Keith and the songs that he played on. In fact I can actually imagine Keith playing on certain Slade songs; maybe songs like 'Far Far Away' or 'Cum On Feel The Noize', only I think he would play a lot

Left: Don Powell drumming with Slade in 1973.

wilder than me.

"I first saw The Who at the Top Rank Ballroom in Wolverhampton. 'My Generation' had just come out. Noddy [Holder] and myself went to see them. There wasn't that many people there. I watched Keith and he was phenomenal. It struck me then that he played his drums like a lead instrument and everything that he did fitted. And during that show everyone's eyes were glued to Keith Moon.

"I was playing drums by then and the band was just getting going, playing pub gigs, weddings and youth clubs. But seeing Keith that night just floored me. I watched him and he never let up for a second. His drumming was relentless. I wasn't used to this style of drumming. I had cut my teeth listening to the drummers who played behind people like Eddie Cochran and Buddy Holly but Keith was nothing like them.

"I only ever met Keith once. It was in the early seventies and Slade were taken down to the nightclub called Tramp. Keith was in there with Marianne Faithfull, and a few others. We all sat

Keith in 1966 with one of his Premier kits.

around this long table and he was like a naughty schoolboy. We kept making eye contact and we pranked about like two little kids at the back of the class. We got chatting and then at the end of the night, just as he was on his way out, he threw a handful of fivers on the table and called to the waiter, 'Waiter, buy these boys a drink, they will soon own the place.' And then he walked out.

"I heard a story from one of the guys from 10cc, who bought one of Keith's houses. He was walking around the house and the grounds and he spotted a Roller sitting at the bottom of the pool. He got to a phone and called Keith to tell him what he had found to which Keith replied, 'Dear boy, I wondered what happened to that'.

"I think Keith was like a naughty little schoolboy just having fun. He was charming, he wasn't aggressive or out to hurt people. I remember hearing the news about Keith's death and I was frightened. It really did frighten me and it was like, 'Oh bloody hell.' I thought it was such a waste and such a loss of a great talent. There were a lot of people who went around that time and I think some expected Keith to be one of the first to go, but he wasn't. I think the media painted an inaccurate picture and I believe Keith was more in control than what people think."

Left: Keith's 'Pictures of Lily' kit, designed and made for him by Premier Drums in 1967. Above: Keith's Rolls-Royce in the lake at Tara, his house in Chertsey. The house was later sold to Kevin Godley of 10cc, who discovered the car.

MICK AVORY

THE KINKS

"When I started playing drums I was listening to jazz and then it was rock'n'roll. I was in a skiffle band for about three years and then I got a few lessons from a jazz drummer. I was of the same generation as Keith and it was only jazz drummers who gave lessons at the time. I was never going to match the ability of those drummers though so when the R&B scene came along I found that suited my style of drumming better. I had a brush in with The Rolling Stones too, but I didn't play at the gig that I am supposed to have done. But I did rehearse with them a couple of times. Instead I went on to join The Kinks at the beginning of 1964.

"It was once I was drumming with The Kinks and we were touring, doing the package tours and club circuit, that I got to know The Who. I saw Keith when he was in The High Numbers. I thought he was a mad drummer and he didn't go unnoticed. Keith didn't impress me with his technique, but his flair of how he played the music did. He also looked good when he played because of his flailing arms. Keith played very differently to me. I played more organised patterns but Keith didn't. He was a lot more free and did some amazing rolls and flicked his sticks all over the place. Keith didn't want to be disciplined, he wanted to be free. Keith was a natural showman.

"The Who had a really big sound for a four-piece, and how Keith played fitted the band perfectly. What Keith did was just get up and play; his drumming parts came to him naturally. He didn't seem to worry about things like paradiddles and things like that. What Keith did was bring drummers to the fore again, just like Gene Krupa had done in the old days. What he had was natural flair and originality and that worked for him and The Who.

"I don't think Keith needed drummers' rules in his life. I doubt he would have understood them. I'm sure he had patterns in his head, but I doubt they were formed the way usual drummers do; using bars and embellishments. He just wasn't that organised.

"When I didn't see Keith on the road I would see him down the various clubs in London. I'm sure he did have a sensible side but he didn't show it very often. I think he felt that he had to live up to his reputation. I think he had to do stupid things because he felt people expected it from him. I saw Keith do some stupid things in the Speakeasy but the management never threw him out; if anything they expected this behaviour. If Keith had lived on to be my age now he wouldn't still be doing it; he wouldn't be able to. It didn't surprise me when I heard about Keith's death. He was never going to make old bones. Keith was of a time when lots of people took lots of things and they weren't that cautious about it. That's the way life was and that's the way Keith was; and he played drums that way too. Keith got all the success and notoriety but it burned him out."

Left: The natural showman, Keith in 1964 in an early publicity photo.

JACK BRUCE

CREAM

"The first thing that springs to my mind when I think of Keith is being on his hovercraft and driving around the grounds of his house Tara; and Keith slamming on the breaks just before we hit the glass doors.

"I wasn't that aware of The Who because we worked in the south-west of London, whereas they worked in the north-west. That seemed like a long way away so our paths never crossed. I only met Keith around 1967 when we did the 'Murray the K' show in New York. It was an amazing show that had them and us and people like Wilson Pickett on it.

Ferocious is one word that I would use to describe Keith's drumming and he was a great drummer for The Who. I would say that he was the sort of drummer that couldn't play with a lot of other bands, but for The Who he was superb. Keith developed his own style that he had modelled around the songs of The Who. Because of this it didn't matter if he sped it up or slowed it down in some particular point; it was his thing to do that. You could apply the same thing to Ginger [Baker], but then you could also apply that to many drummers of many great bands.

"I don't think Keith was the only pioneering drummer from that time; I think there were a few. I mean when I was playing with Ginger before Cream he played the way he did then, just with more jazz style. But there were a handful of drummers around, which included Keith and Ginger, that were pioneering something different. Those guys didn't rely on the technical sort of drumming, although

Keith was technical in his own way.

"Keith and I played along together a little bit. I can't remember exactly when but we would find ourselves in the same recording sessions and do something informally. I found some tapes in my attic recently that I thought I had lost; so yeah, I think there'll be some recordings of me and Keith playing together laying around somewhere. It was some stuff I did with Tony Williams and John McLaughlin. Those playing sessions with Keith would have been around that period when The Who was recording 'Magic Bus'. This was when we were mostly hanging out together and this came about because Leslie West had properly introduced us to each other.

"Keith was the funniest guy ever. He couldn't be anything else, he was just so funny and he'd have you laughing so much. I'm pretty funny too and we would just be laughing non-stop. We couldn't just sit down and have a chat, we had to laugh instead. I think we used to get on Townshend's nerves quite a bit the way we would show up at Who recording sessions and be the way we were.

"Through the seventies I didn't see that much of Keith. We were both off doing our own things and he was living in the States a lot. But we did run into each other from time to time and it was always good to see each other.

"Keith Moon is not a character that you can forget and it's been a hell of a long time since he died. I wouldn't say it came as a shock when I heard about him dying, but it was terrible news. The thing was, we had all seen him 'going for it' and he wasn't really looking after himself. But everyone knows all the stories."

Keith and his hovercraft in the lake at the Crystal Palace Bowl, Saturday 3 June 1972.

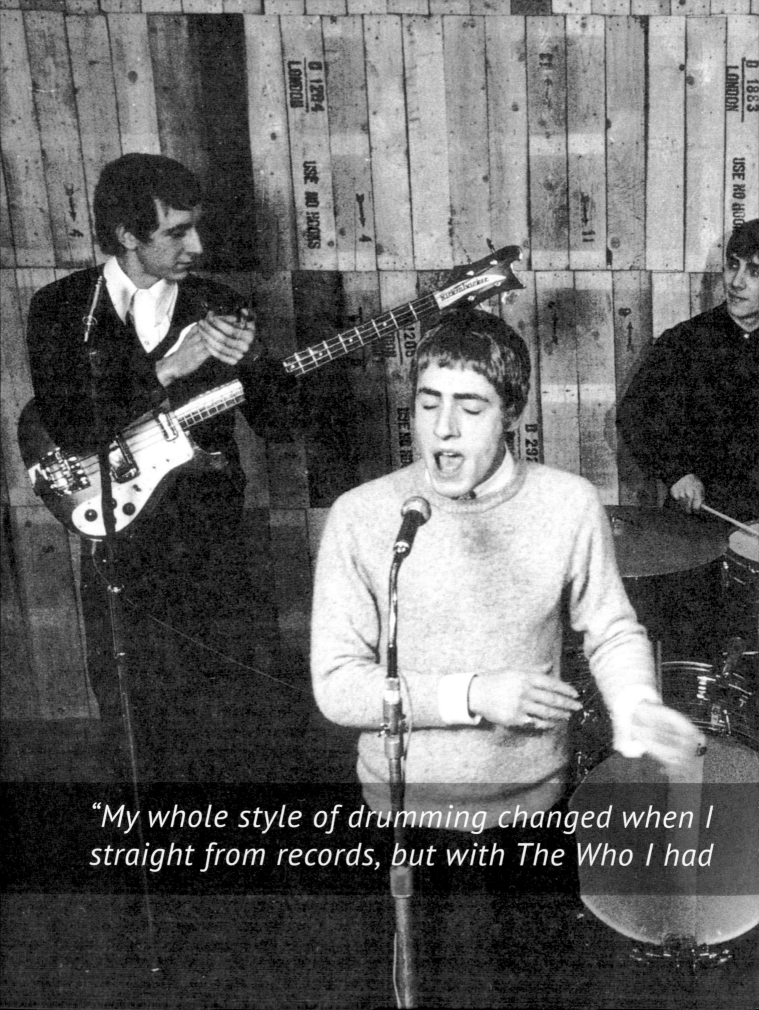

"My whole style of drumming changed when I
straight from records, but with The Who I had

joined the band. Before I had just been copying to develop a style of my own."

CARL PALMER

EMERSON, LAKE & PALMER

"*What immediately comes to mind when I think of Keith is the sixties and that great song 'I Can't Explain'.* That was one of The Who's early songs and a song that helped define a generation. It was the beginning of the Mods and Rockers and The Who were the Mods.

"For me The Who and Keith Moon represent the very first rock band (that were in the charts) that I ever saw live. They were playing in my hometown at the Aston University [*28 January 1966 – Ed.*]. I was only about 14 at the time and they left a big impression on me.

"As time went by I got to meet all of The Who band members because I was in a group called The Crazy World of Arthur Brown and they were on Track Records, the same as The Who. Because of this I got to tour with The Who in 1968. It was a very exciting moment to be on the same record label and under the same management.

"It was during that period of meeting the band and hanging out with people like Roger, Pete and John (John was a favourite bass player of mine) that I got to know Keith reasonably well. He helped me out on tour on a couple of occasions. I broke one of my bass drum pedals and asked Keith if he could help me out. He asked to see the broken pedal and we had a laugh about it. He was very nice and not the crazy chap that he was known to be; he was very down to earth. He told me to follow him and took me to a van that was parked outside. It was full of drums and spare parts. He opened a tea-chest and it was packed with Premier pedals. 'Take two, dear boy', he said, which I did and used for the rest of the tour. At the end of the tour I went to see Keith with the pedals and thanked

him for the loan. Keith wouldn't let me return them and said, 'You have them on me'. So I kept them. He even said if I wanted any help getting a deal with Premier he would look into it. I found Keith to be a lovely guy, a great man and an absolute gentleman. It was a shame he got caught up in the rock world and it did catch up with him.

"The thing is, Keith wasn't a great drummer (with technique), let's be honest. What Keith was, was a completely original drummer and when someone is a completely original drummer, that is a great drummer. He made The Who work. He didn't need to keep time; that wasn't his game, he had Entwistle to do that. In my mind Keith was the Elvin Jones of rock drummers; that's how I would describe him.

"No one did away with the hi-hats like Keith and no one tried to keep time like Keith; these were the things that made him original. When he did drum fills they were sensational and he added an element of excitement. He added an orchestration to the songs that only he could have done. What Keith did was blasé and avant garde and that's what he was like and he made it work and he made it his own. Keith contributed a big part to the sound of The Who because of his originality.

"Sometime after Keith's death I ended up playing on the album that Roger Daltrey put together for Keith Moon when he died called *Under A Raging Moon*. He asked various drummers to play on it and I was asked. After Keith died I offered my services to drum for The Who; I think they had a tour organised or something, but they took some time off before getting Kenney in. If I had got the job it wouldn't have been an easy part and it wouldn't have been easy to copy Keith's style. I was pleased to be asked by Roger to play on the album though."

The Who

the crazy world of Arthur Brown

Personal Management:

CHRIS STAMP—KIT LAMBERT
New Action Management
58 Old Compton Street
London, England

Publicity Management:

ROGERS, COWAN & BRENNER
398 Madison Ave.
New York, New York
Phone: (212) 759-6272

PREMIER TALENT ASSOCIATES, INC. 200 WEST 57th STREET NEW YORK, N. Y.
TEL. (212) 757-4300

NEAL SMITH

ALICE COOPER

"I was lucky to meet Keith Moon and did so several times; just a couple of guys hanging out and drinking beer. There really was nobody like Keith and I'm pleased to have been asked to be included in this book. When we were recording the *Billion Dollar Babies* album in Morgan Studios in London, Keith came to visit. The studio had a bar right there; I dunno how good an idea that was. One time I was having a beer with Keith and Marc Bolan. Keith got pretty out if it; I think he'd been drinking brandy before he arrived. He did his Robert Newton impression of Blackbeard over and again. I've never seen anyone do a greater impersonation; he had the look, the eyes and the

voice. That same night Marc Bolan was trying to talk Keith into setting up a group with him. I thought it was the dumbest fucking idea that I had ever heard. I loved T. Rex but what could Keith do on a Marc Bolan type of song?

"We were in Morgan Studios in 1972 but I had met Keith Moon and The Who before that. The Who were playing at the Rainbow Theatre. We also played and did our *School's Out* show. After the show we went to see The Who in the changing rooms. We got shown into a room and I saw Pete and I introduced myself, 'Hi Pete I'm Neal from Alice Cooper', and he replied, 'I know who you fucking are' and leaned down and bit me on the knee. I thought that was interesting and something that I'd miss about the English culture, 'the biting of the knee greeting'. Then I introduced myself to Keith and he was great and we chatted.

"But even before that Rainbow Theatre show Alice Cooper opened for them in Detroit; only I didn't get to meet Keith that night. But I did hear about something that is especially special to me. The venue we played in was an old theatre and had a giant pull-down screen. The opening band would set up in front of the screen and the main band behind. If you stood behind the screen and the lights were up you could see through the screen; but from out front all you see are the lights or whatever is being projected onto it. Our last song of the set was 'Black JuJu'. When I came off stage my roadie, whose name was Goose, grabbed me and said, 'Hey boss, did you see what was going on?' I said, 'What do you mean Goose?' He then explained to me that Keith Moon was on his drums behind the screen playing along to 'Black JuJu' at the same time as me. He said that the view from the side of the stage was incredible because he could see both

Keith as Robert Newton's Blackbeard in The Kids Are Alright.

Keith and me on our drums playing along together. And I never knew. Goose said Keith was like a mirror image of me and I'm all over my drums in that song (inspired by Keith Moon).

"I joined Alice Cooper in late 1967 when the band was still called Nazz. I was already inspired by Keith's drumming and this was further contributed to by a bad car accident (Good Friday morning 1968) that involved the Alice Cooper band. I had seen Keith playing with two bass drums and I wanted that too. I had seen Ginger Baker using two bass drums too, and they were my two big inspirations. It was after the car accident that I had the opportunity to rebuild my equipment and I added a second bass drum. Up until this point I had a set of Rogers drums; a standard size kit (bass drum, floor tom and two tom-toms). I then bought a Ludwig set, which was the same size as the Rogers and put both kits together to make one big kit. I just stripped all the veneer off the shells and then hand-painted them, which Alice and Dennis helped with; they are both great artists. My later drums I painted pink, which looked like something out of a baby's nursery. It was kind of inspired by Keith's 'Pictures of Lily' drum kit.

"I never got to play Keith's kit but I did see Keith play them in 1968. And that was and still is one of the most phenomenal shows that I have ever seen in my life. During 'Magic Bus' Keith was up at the front of the stage playing claves and then just as Pete Townshend went to play the big power chords Keith jumped over the drum set and just started playing away and then the song took off like a rocket. And talk about dynamic. Keith had great

Alice Cooper and Keith, Malibu, 1976.

dynamics. I think dynamics is what's missing in music today. Keith was an expert at knowing when to hold back and then take off.

"I first heard about The Who when I was in Phoenix [Arizona]. My mother belonged to the *Reader's Digest* and she would get books. She also knew that I was really interested in the bands that were coming over to America during the British Invasion period. I came home from school one day and there was a package waiting for me. I opened it up and it was The Who's first album, *The Who Sings My Generation*. Around this time others were also getting to know about The Who and the band was getting 'My Generation' played on the radio. I remember driving to a band rehearsal with my band mates and the song came on the radio. We listened to Roger Daltrey's stuttering and Keith Moon's insane drumming and we were all laughing hysterically. When I first got to see The Who on stage I had to laugh just like I had done in the car that day. It was a real 'what the fuck' moment and it just all worked. What Keith played was very unorthodox but it worked.

"Hearing Keith Moon play drums for the first time was a life changing thing. Up until that point I hadn't heard anything like it. I couldn't have expected to hear anything like it. I mean every drummer up to that point when Keith Moon arrived had just been a glorified metronome.

"I had grown up listening to Gene Krupa, Sandy Nelson and Buddy Rich, and they were all great, and then I heard Charlie Watts and Ringo, then out of nowhere came Keith Moon. So there was this more exciting drummer with two bass drums and more energy than a volcano and he's not missing a beat and is right on everything. It sounded like organised chaos and it worked. He was like 'one with the drums'. When Keith sat behind his drums he was like fusing with them. Keith's drums wanted him to play them the way he did.

"Thinking about Keith Moon's drumming excites me still today. I was very sad when he left us. I mean forget the stuff with the cars and the pools and all that kinda crazy stuff; that's rock'n'roll, but what Keith did as a drummer on stage, to me is the equivalent of what Mozart did with composing. Keith was just genius. He is the most exciting drummer that will ever be. I equate what Keith Moon did with drums to what Jimi Hendrix did with the guitar.

"I listen to John Bonham and there are things that he does that I just can't do. I just don't have John's feel for them. And then I know there are drummers who have tried but can't play parts on the *Billion Dollar Babies* album. And Keith had that whole special touch and feel thing. He had a great sprinkling of insanity that helped give him that unique sound and style. You can even see it in the expression in Keith's face when he played. He would attack the fucking hell out of them drums and then he would back off a little; then pounce again. He was like a big lion playing with a little mouse. No one handled the sticks like Keith Moon. I think he has been so under-appreciated. And you can't underestimate what there is to learn from Keith's playing. From early on my attitude was always 'Fuck everybody... I'm going to do whatever I want (and I was given this opportunity in Alice Cooper)' and I got this spirit from Keith Moon.

"I saw The Who after Keith had died and it was still amazing. I remembering saying to myself, 'Why do I listen to any other music?' The Who really are responsible for the best rock music ever recorded. Even seeing The Who a couple of years back was still phenomenal. I mean they brought in videos of Keith and John; it was beyond a tribute. I met Zak Starkey that night and in fact the drums on the sleeve of my *KillSmith And The Greenfire Empire* album actually belonged to Zak Starkey from that night. I think Keith Moon has influenced hundreds of thousands of drummers and he is much missed."

DENNIS 'MACHINE GUN' THOMPSON

MC5

"MC5 had just formed when 'My Generation' was released. At the time the MC5 were working on developing our own style of full-blast rock'n'roll. I was still in the 11th grade and also working a part-time job in downtown Detroit. It was a night job. After one night's work I was driving home down the expressway listening to the radio and on comes 'My Generation'. Before the first minute of the song had finished I was just going crazy. I was playing along to the drums on the steering wheel and I was getting a real kick out of it. I had to pull off the freeway and crank the radio up to 10 and I went nuts. Then when Moon exploded and did his single stroke roll at the end of the song I said, 'Oh my god, here he is, finally someone has broken the barrier of drummers just playing in the pocket'. I sat in my car, wetting my panties like a 13-year-old girl. I just knew then that Moon had opened the door for the drummers in rock'n'roll. He changed everything for me. It was beautiful.

"It was great to hear the way Moon played along to Pete Townshend and the way Pete used feedback guitar. The MC5 were just starting to use

MC5, left to right: Dennis 'Machine Gun' Thompson, Wayne Kramer, Fred 'Sonic' Smith and Rob Tyner perform live in 1969 in Mount Clemens, Michigan. Note Thompson's twin bass drums, the same as Keith's.

feedback too. The Who and the MC5 were on the same plane; but The Who were two years ahead of us. After hearing 'My Generation' on the radio I went and bought the first album and played it until the grooves were worn out.

"When I listened to music and I liked the drummer I would study him. You can call it research or mentoring or you can call it stealing. This is what I did with The Who and Keith Moon. The Who were my number one band, which was great because a little bit down the road the MC5 were playing at the Grande Ballroom, it's a bit like the Fillmore but in Detroit. Now Detroit is a tough city, very industrial, very hard-working and very hard-partying. The MC5 got to play at the Grande Ballroom almost every weekend. We did this for free because we were trying to help attract customers. Eventually more national bands like Janis Joplin, Cream and Led Zeppelin came to Detroit.

"We included in our set lots of songs that we had liked from the invasion of the British bands like The Animals and The Kinks. We just lifted songs that we liked and played them. We even did our own version of 'My Generation'. We were still at a time when we were earning our bones and getting our chops together. The audience recognised lots of the songs and just went fucking bananas, and at the end of our set we just smashed our equipment. The crowd loved us and our 'high energy' music. At the time other bands called their music a 'rave up' but we called ours 'high energy'. It's what happens when a band just goes for it. That's why we used to say 'kick out the jams motherfuckers or get off the stage'. We didn't want any weak-arse music like they were playing in California.

"Nowadays the MC5 are becoming legendary for their pioneering aspect but Keith's drumming was that too. There are a lot of writers that seem only interested in Keith's sensationalist aspect and they miss the serious side. Keith Moon was a great pioneer. I remember watching Keith play from the wings at the Grande and he was for me the complete rock'n'roll drummer. He had a great show. He was the centre-piece of The Who. Moon was flashy and explosive and really drove The Who. They were never the same after he passed away.

"Keith Moon changed my life and my drumming style. In fact I had to make an important decision. My father was going to put me through college. He worked two jobs to pay for three of us to go through school. My older brother and sister had been offered college by my dad but they had declined; I accepted. But in my second year the MC5 said to me that we were about to get signed and go on the road and if I wanted to stay in the band I couldn't stay at college. I left college and I have to blame Keith Moon and The Who because I elected to stay with the band and play drums. It broke my dad's heart at the start but over the years he got over it and he understood. But you see, The Who personified what rock'n'roll was all about and should be about, and that's what I wanted.

"Now that I'm a little older and a little wiser I just have three bands that stick with me, who I think are the greatest. I put The Who on top, Jimi Hendrix is second and the John Coltrane Quartet comes next. My three favourite drummers of all time are Keith Moon, Mitch Mitchell and Elvin Jones. If you could study those three drummers you'd be one hell of a great drummer."

Right: The Who on the 1968 US tour, with what looks like sprays of water coming off Keith's drum heads.

RICHARD BARNES

FORMER FLATMATE OF PETE TOWNSHEND AND AUTHOR OF

THE WHO: MAXIMUM R&B

"What started off as a hobby for Keith and the other members of The Who quickly became more than that; it took up most of their time. They weren't on a wage as such but they were getting paid for the gigs that they played. It was only when they changed the name from The Detours to The Who that I realised they were really serious about what they were doing. At least Pete was looking for something bigger.

"Now, before Keith it was Doug Sandom, and I knew Doug well and still do, we have always naturally gotten on well together. And I was at the Zanzibar Club on the occasion when Pete [Townshend] had a go at him. I was shocked and thought it was unfair and out of order. But what was being pointed out was that Doug was from a different generation to the rest of us. He was a few years older than us and not part of what was happening. So once Doug left and Keith joined what I noticed was the difference that made and the difference can only be described as amazing.

"I certainly wasn't in a position to judge whether Doug had been a good drummer or not. Around that time I would go and see a lot of the bands playing like The Yardbirds and The Kinks, and they all had 'their' drummers who played a certain way. Those drummers seemed more to just do their job, keeping the beat. But Keith Moon wasn't like any of them. He was a fun drummer and instead of him just providing a background noise he supplied an instant driving force; and he had the beginnings of this even before he developed it within The Who. He was the only drummer around who'd hit the drums as hard and as loud and as sharp. And this was very different to Doug Sandom and all the other drummers that The Detours auditioned. And when Moon played people watched. You couldn't take your eyes off of him. He was a one man show playing at the back of The Who and driving them along at the same time. What Moon brought to the band made the band sound different and it worked. When Keith got behind his drums he was like a kid who had just been given a drum kit for Christmas. He took to playing the drums and being in bands so naturally.

"Over the years I got to see both sides of Moon but his part behind a drum kit was sublime and amazing. He could be outrageous and even more so after he'd taken some pills but he'd still manage to produce some incredible drum fills and rolls, that shouldn't have normally worked, but he somehow made them work. He was a show-off and he was wonderful to watch.

"When Keith played his drumming sped up and slowed down but it didn't really matter because he had John Entwistle to keep it together and Pete Townshend simply got used to it, he was aware of it, but he just got on with it. I think from the first time that they heard Moon play they understood what they were going to get, and they realised he had something special and they stuck with him. Moon worked in The Who, which was just as well really because he couldn't have gone out and worked as a session drummer.

Left: A very youthful Keith drumming at the Locarno, Stevenage, 14 July 1965.

"I remember the Moon that first joined The Who. He was actually very shy. He still showed off in many ways but he was very much the junior member of the band. He looked much younger than he was in the early days. He lost his looks as time went by.

"Pete and I inherited a bunch of albums. Tom Wright was such a gift to The Who. He gave us 250 blues albums and we listened to them over and over. Jimmy Reed was always playing in our flat. But then you had Keith Moon who was totally into surfing music. Moon and Townshend were like chalk and cheese. We liked surf music and would get them out once every few weeks, but Keith played them every day. We had The Beach Boys but for us they didn't compare to Howlin' Wolf. They did later with *Pet Sounds*. But Keith on the other hand thought that album was rubbish and a betrayal.

"One of the biggest influences on The Who were Johnny Kid & The Pirates. They were a great British band at a time when there were lots of third rate- American copying bands playing the circuit. But somehow Keith had really got into the surf music. I had never met such a surfing freak as Moonie. When Keith lived in Tara House I stayed with him. I went to a club with him and went back to Tara and then didn't leave for about nine months. I had an in joke where I'd say I was going to dig a tunnel and get out. Then someone would say have another gin and tonic!

"At Tara House Keith had rooms that only ever played music. It was just so Moon and so mad. In the rooms he had cassette machines that played whatever tape was in it on a loop. In one room he only had Beatles playing, in another room it was Beach Boys and the next Jan & Dean, and the music was always playing really loudly. Now Jan & Dean had one awful song that had loads of dreadful laughing on it. Moonie loved it and would laugh along with it. He must have been the only person in the world who loved that song. He was mad on it. And he was great to be around."

Keith at Tara, his house in St Ann's Hill, Chertsey, 1973.

RICK BUCKLER

THE JAM

"The Jam's 'Down In The Tube Station' was released in October 1978. At the time we didn't have a B-side in mind. And then we heard the news about Keith Moon. Paul, Bruce and I decided it would be a fitting idea to do a version of 'So Sad About Us'. It wasn't a song we had done before so we had to go off and learn it. We liked the song for the lyric 'so sad about us' and we saw it as being a fitting tribute with regards to Moon's passing.

"I had been as stunned by the news of his death as the next person. I think a lot of people thought that someday something like this would happen to him. He appeared to be on that self-destruct path; like so many others from the sixties and seventies.

"I admired Keith Moon as a drummer even though he wasn't really my sort of drummer; his drumming, like his life, seemed close to the edge. I had a conversation once with the managing director of Premier Drums. He told me that there would be boxes of drums sitting on the side of the stage, waiting and ready to replace the ones that Moonie would break throughout a show.

"He told me that Moonie would do the most outrageous things on stage; for example he would go to do a drum fill and those looking on would think to themselves he is never going to make it round the drums in time, but he would go for it anyway. He was like a man sitting in a wheelchair spinning on one wheel and it was as if he could fall over at any time.

"I think most of Keith Moon's drumming sounded like he was pretty much on the edge and this I did like, it kind of put a tension into things. But discipline wise, I just don't think he planned anything, he simply just went for it and that was the type of person and character he was. Playing drums is really just an extension of your personality and you can see Moonie's in his playing. I'm just not like that. If I don't think I can pull off a drum fill in the time available, I just avoid trying it. That's me. I like to have things well-rehearsed as much as possible and be in control. I try to play within my limits, I know not to push it too far because if I do I'll know that you run the risk of falling off. I see it as a scale from one to 10 and if you know your limitations are at nine, then don't push it to 10. It keeps things safe with less chance of making a mistake. I think Keith Moon was always on 10 and pushing for 11."

[Reproduced with kind permission of Rick from his autobiography That's Entertainment.]

Roger, Keith and Pete at the Duke of York's Barracks, Kings Road, Chelsea, Saturday 12 November 1966. They were filmed performing five songs, clips of which were broadcast in a special 'Swinging London' edition of the Today *show on NBC TV in the US.*

STEVE WHITE

STYLE COUNCIL / PAUL WELLER / TRIO VALORE

"Energy, originality, one of a kind, a complete innovator and somebody who had a unique voice on a drum set! Keith Moon is certainly right up there alongside Ringo as my favourite pop drummer. I think the early run of Who singles were classics. I can still hear influences like Chuck Berry in those songs and the way Keith plays a swing ride cymbal. A lot of drummers from the Chuck Berry-type bands had that beautiful swing ride and Keith had it too, at least in the early days. Personally I think some of the later stuff and all the excess was a bit boring. But the early stuff and the complete innovation that he was bringing to the drums was great, and he was a total unsettled spirit.

"Keith came out of a time when most of the drummers were controlled by a very conservative music scene. But then a band like The Who came along. The Who had that special combination of fire, earth, air and water; which all the great bands have had. Keith was allowed to breathe the fire and allowed to not be held back and restrained, which he would be now, like drummers tend to be. Fortunately for Keith he was allowed to play straight from the heart.

"I know that Keith did study how to play drums in his early day. Carlo Little taught him, but he didn't allow that to get in his way of playing with pure unadulterated joy. This was the stuff that was so great about Keith Moon and I would have loved to hear Keith Moon play with someone like Miles Davis. That would have been amazing to see.

"I remember the first time I heard Keith Moon's drumming. I had a copy of 'My Generation' in a box of singles that my uncle gave me. Also in that box of 45s were records by The Small Faces and The Beatles. That box of records pretty much became my early bible of pop music. I put 'My Generation' on my little old brown Dansette and it was like 'Wow, what is this?' I was struck by the way the cymbal just kinda propelled the whole track along. There was very little playing to the back beat. Keith was playing along more to the vocal, but as well as playing for the song, he was playing for himself too and I really liked that. Hearing Keith playing on 'My Generation' literally did blow me away.

"Keith wasn't a jazz drummer but sometimes he would almost play like a jazz drummer; especially the way he put fills and rolls into unusual places. He was very skilled at accenting along with Roger's vocals, or playing off John's bass line or Pete's guitar. And at that time Pete was such a unique guitarist too. It must have been a drummer's dream. It's the sort of chemistry that you cannot make in a laboratory; what they had in The Who was a natural meeting of something that only happens very rarely. I mean other examples would be Mitch Mitchell with Jimi or Lennon and McCartney. And The Who's songs were absolutely perfect for Keith's drumming.

"I had done some stuff with Roger and the Teenage Cancer Trust, then a mutual friend called Angie put us in touch again. At this point I had only met John but never Pete. Angie called me to tell me there was going to be a concert and that turned out to be *Live8*. Like *Live Aid* which I had played in with the Style Council, it came around very quickly, and before we knew it, the concert was upon us.

"Damon Minchella and myself were asked if we'd be interested in playing for The Who. Of course we jumped at the chance, and then it all went quiet and we didn't really hear much more until very near the time. We were doing some recording with Paul Weller at his Solid Bond Studios in London and Pete Townshend came in and asked us if we were still up for doing it. We said we were. Pete then gave us a list of five songs and asked us to learn them. And then we didn't actually get together to rehearse the songs until one or two days before the concert.

"At that point it was decided that the two songs to be played would be 'Won't Get Fooled Again' and 'Who Are You'. We all got together for the rehearsal and I took along my Premier red sparkle kit. Roger was already waiting and Pete arrived quite late. He literally picked up his guitar and we launched into the first song. At the end he turned to Roger and said, 'I think we'll do the two songs the other way round at the concert' and then he was gone.

"But just before he left Pete came over to my drum kit and looked at it. My kit was a replica of the kit Keith Moon used back in 1966. Pete leaned out his hand and gave it a gentle touch and said, 'Red sparkle. I like red sparkle.' And then he left.

"We went to *Live8* and Damon and I pretty much stuck together. The rest of The Who guys, like Simon Townshend, were all good guys, but there was no Roger or Pete. We didn't actually see them two until we walked out onto the stage.

"I plugged in my in-ear monitors (which I hate) but they weren't working. And at that point no one seemed to want to take responsibility to get them working. To say the world dropped out of my bottom was an understatement. I mean I was on stage with The Who and my ear monitor wasn't working.

"Now luckily for me the comedian Peter Kay was given 30 seconds to do a bit on the stage and introduce The Who. I had met Peter via my wife previously so I knew there'd be no way he would stick to just 30 seconds. And he did over-run and in that time I managed to get the ear monitors working. The sound engineers turned in the frequency and I remember hearing Pete say to Bobby Pridden, 'Fuck off, Charlie Drake' and as he said it my inner ear pieces burst into life, and it was the most surreal moment in my entire career.

"During 'Won't Get Fooled Again' I remember dropping down to the part where it's just the keyboard sequencers and looking up to the sky and thinking, 'Keith, if you're up there, give me a heads up on this one buddy'. I was shitting myself because I had been told that if Roger likes what's happening he will do the scream at the end, but if he isn't feeling it, he won't. But he did the scream and it was fucking great. And it was only when we left the stage that I spoke to Roger and Pete. Pete said 'nice one' and then he was gone again. I had no real idea whether they had liked it or not liked it. I just told myself that we did it and did our best. I grabbed a beer and as I did, Pink Floyd started to play 'Comfortably Numb' and I thought, 'This whole thing has been a rock'n'roll moment'. Much later I read Pete's autobiography and he mentioned that he did like the performance, so that's okay.

"I remember that I looked at the footage on YouTube and read the comments. That was the last time I've ever read any comments on such sites about any performance that I've ever done. Most of the comments from that Who performance were great but then I read one where someone wrote some unpleasant stuff along the lines of 'Who's that on the drums?' And then it hit me; I realised the enormity of what I had done. But I didn't try to play like Keith—that would have been an insult and that would have been stupid; I can only play like myself and I tried to do those Who songs the best that I could."

Right: Pete: "Red sparkle. I like red sparkle." The Who appearing on Rediffusion TV's Ready Steady Go! *broadcast live from Wembley, 3 December 1965.*

TODD SUCHERMAN

STYX

"**Keith Moon personified rock music in the sixties and seventies.** He had a ferocious, reckless and dangerous attitude that was so unique to him. I wish I had been alive back in 1966 to have seen the birth of that. He was certainly an exciting game-changer.

"When Keith played he had a mix of pure rock'n'roll with a bit of American surf music thrown in and when he played with The Who you were left feeling like there could be a train disaster at any time. Who records were a really exciting listening experience.

"I grew up being the youngest in a musical family and there was always lots of different music being played around the house. But it was *Tommy* that really brought The Who and Keith Moon to my attention. I also saw a copy of *Downbeat* magazine and there was a picture of Keith with his drums and he had two rows of tom-toms and I had never seen that before. I thought, 'Okay what's going on with this guy, this looks a bit over the top?'

"I started to look into Keith Moon and realised that he was totally unique when it came to the way he set his drums up. And then I saw *The Kids Are Alright* and could see his drums close up and hear the way he played, and I had to go and buy a bunch of Who records. It occurred to me that, simply, no one else played like him. And I was left with the idea that he never liked to play the same way twice. Which is really how a lot of jazz musicians think and play, with their constant improvisation. Keith had that sort of spirit too and at that time it was unique in rock music.

"In my opinion there was something about Keith's drumming that was very special between 1970 and 1973. There was something extra about the drumming on albums like *Live At Leeds* and *Who's Next*, and then something seemed to change around the time of *Quadrophenia*. I think *Quadrophenia* showed the first signs of the sluggishness that would sadly come later.

"And it bugs me out when someone says that Keith Moon didn't groove, but they're wrong. There were tons of songs where Keith laid down a great groove: 'Join Together', 'Put The Money Down' and 'Relay' for example. Keith was also one of, if not the first, to play along to backing tracks. He did this on songs like 'Baba O'Riley' and 'Won't Get Fooled Again'. It's common nowadays but back then it wasn't.

"I'm not surprised that there is still so much interest in a drummer like Keith Moon. I think some of his over-the-top antics overshadowed some of his drumming but he will be remembered for his drumming and as such a unique and endearing character on and off stage. This will continue for decades. It's hard for any drummer or any musician to have their own unique voice on their instrument, but Keith Moon did and he developed it too, and while he did he brought the drums out front and gave drummers the permission to be a lead instrument too. Keith Moon and The Who will stand the test of time."

"I gotta get runnin' now!" Keith drumming and singing 'Bell Boy' on the 1973 Quadrophenia *tour.*

PETER 'DOUGAL' BUTLER

KEITH MOON'S PERSONAL ASSISTANT, 1971–1977

"A good drummer and mayhem is what first springs to mind when I think of Keith. I never tired of watching him play drums. He was fantastic and a world of his own. Before I worked for Keith I saw him playing with The Beachcombers. They were supporting Shane Fenton & The Fentones. This was in church hall in Hayes in the early sixties. I think he must have only just turned 16 years old, if that. That was the first time I clapped eyes on him and he was a good drummer then.

"Even then he had his own style and that made him stand out. And then his style developed even more as he played with The Who. There was only three instruments in The Who and what Keith did was he played a lead part in that arrangement. He wasn't just a 'keeping time' drummer, he was very much up front. I called it orchestra playing. It was like an orchestra playing, with stuff going on all over the place. And I mean that in the nicest possible way.

"I remember that we done a tour in the States in 1972 and I was told that in the two hours that he played on stage, that was as much work as a lumberjack does in a week. He had a remarkable amount of energy. He used to wear Chelsea boots and at the end of a show there would be puddles of sweat that would fall out of them.

"All the time that I knew him he never rehearsed or practised. He never owned a practice kit. The only time Keith rehearsed was with the band in the studio or when they prepared to go on a tour.

"As a drummer he didn't push himself to become a great drummer. He would never say that he was the best drummer. And what he did have was a great deal of respect for other drummers and it didn't matter what style they played, whether it was jazz or R&B, it didn't matter to him nor did it

Left: Keith and Dougal at John Lennon's beach house, Malibu 1974. In the background Linda McCartney, John Lennon and Paul McCartney, the first time in each other's company since The Beatles' split. Right: Keith and Dougal indoors at Malibu. Far right: Dougal and Keith.

matter if another drummer was thought of as being good or bad. He simply had total respect. There could be no comparing him to John Bonham or Ginger Baker because they played different styles to Keith. I can remember John Bonham being in awe of Keith Moon. There was one gig where this young guy was in the dressing room hanging about and wanting to see and speak to Keith. In the end I had to ask him to leave. It turned out to be John Bonham. A few years later when Keith and John played together at the Forum in LA it was magic. John told me that it had been one of the highlights of his career, he told me it had been one of the 'ultimate thrills of my life'.

"Keith didn't not practice because he was lazy or anything like that. He was a natural drummer and the way he played with The Who suited him and the band. He plugged a lot of gaps in The Who songs with his drum fills. He was absolutely brilliant and often unbelievable. Keith Moon and a drum kit were meant to be.

"I have never known a drummer to play like Keith and it doesn't surprise me that even after all these years since he passed away there's still so much interest in him. He has left us a huge legacy. I go to Who concerts now and there's teenage kids wearing parkas and tee-shirts and they all know Keith Moon and many of them weren't even born when Keith was alive. And any new young drummer finds their way to Keith. Many still take up the drums because of him, because of what they see or hear. And it's not because of the Moon The Loon tag (that I hate), it's because of Keith Moon the drummer. I think if he was still with us he would also be proud of what he has done as a drummer.

"I miss him terribly. From 1967 onwards he and I spent a hell of a lot of time together. I miss him both as a person and a mate. Just to be in his company was a privilege and regardless of whether he was playing drums or not he was a nice person to be around and obviously good fun."

Left: Keith and Dougal at the Edgewater Inn, Seattle, 1971. Right: At the UCLA Film School, Los Angeles in 1977.

Keith and John Entwistle enjoying a little sharpener or two at Tara, Keith's home in Chertsey. Behind them is Dougal in his chauffeur's uniform, standing next to Keith's fully furnished milk float.

'LEGS' LARRY SMITH

THE BONZO DOG DOO-DAH BAND

"Yes, the dear boy. We all know he was an unbelievable, highly original and never-to-be-replaced drummer.
I first saw Keith playing with The Who on *Ready Steady Go!* and within a couple of years we had become very close friends and shared a lot of madness.

Not a lot of people know this but Keith and I were planning a big concert to be held at the Royal Albert Hall. It was an event that was just going to feature drummers. We got our idea from a television programme called *Take Your Pick* that was around in the sixties. On the show there was a pyramid of cubes and contained within each one was a key. What Keith and I wanted to do was build something similar on stage, only instead of a key being contained in the cubes there would be drums. And there would be all sorts of drums and drummers. We were going to get Ginger Baker, African drummers and all the top drummers, and we were just going to play and play and play. We wanted to be able to create some really cool sounds in that drum mountain.

"Unfortunately we didn't get around to doing it. It would have been great and Keith was very keen on presenting all aspects of drumming. He loved drums and he loved playing with The Who. The idea originally came around when we were hanging about in 1969/70. We would hang out a lot down the Speakeasy Club in London and have lots of wonderful ideas of which maybe one in fifty would materialise."

Left and Above: Keith and 'Legs' Larry Smith compering the Garden Party at the Crystal Palace Bowl, Saturday 3 June 1972.

JOHN MAHER

BUZZCOCKS

"When I think of Keith Moon I think chaos, but there's so much more to him than just that. Whenever anyone talks about drummers Keith Moon's name always crops up. I saw some online debates recently and in one was a photo of Keith leaping from the stage and heading straight into the audience, along with some drums. There were various comments from people saying things like, 'This is really stupid, this is sacrilege,' but I think unless you were there to experience what was actually happening and what was going on with The Who, and what the state of music was back in them days, those comments have missed the point completely.

"We have to give credit to Keith Moon for being the first drummer to really go off into a type of chaotic showmanship. But then you have to weigh that up with all the other stuff, his lifestyle and his playing. It's just a shame that he became better known for all the notorious stuff rather than the drumming. He made a unique contribution to The Who and I cannot think of anyone else who played like him.

"He certainly came to my attention when I got into playing the drums. Back then I was into Premier drums and of course Keith Moon used Premier drums. I started playing drums when I was 16. My dad rented a drum kit from a music shop in Manchester and within a few weeks I was playing drums in the Buzzcocks, who were still in their formation period. And once I had my kit I jumped at any opportunity to catch Keith Moon when he appeared on the television. It was a must watch, and not just because of the style of his playing but also the way he acted on stage. But I loved to watch the way he rambled around the kit doing odd-ball drum rolls. And it wasn't random playing at all. I describe Keith Moon's playing as melodic. I think he was very aware of what was going on with Townshend, Entwistle and Daltrey, especially Daltrey. Keith Moon was far from just someone who sat behind a drum kit and went crazy."

Right: Demolition of the Pictures of Lily drum kit, Sweden, 1966.

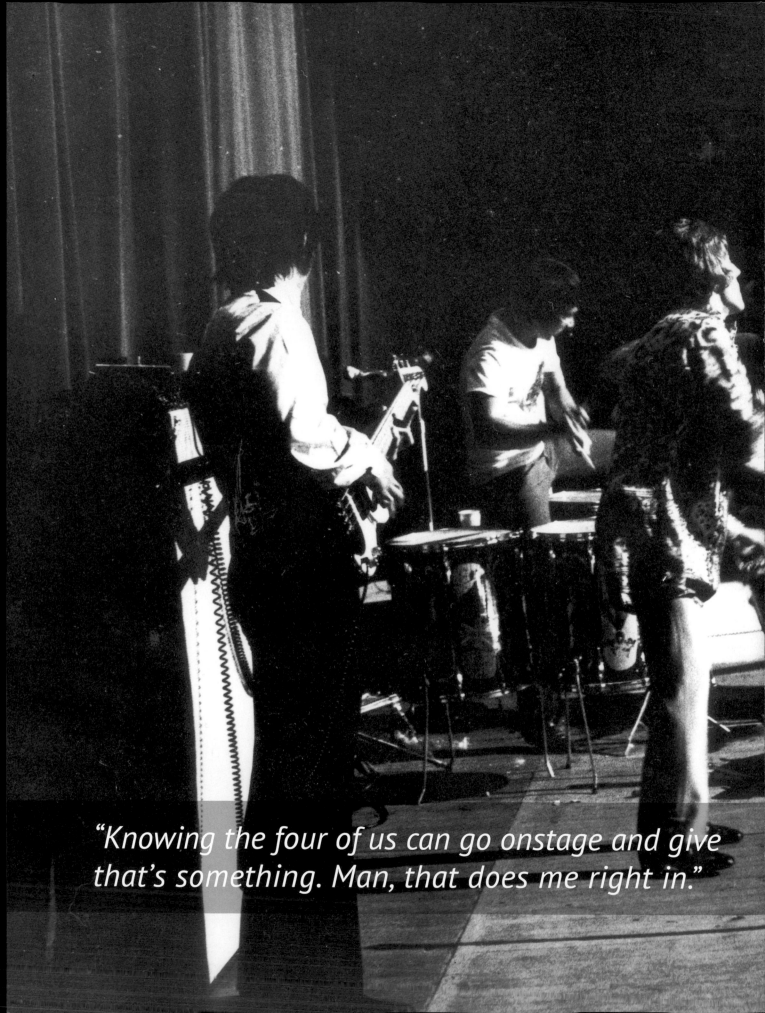

"Knowing the four of us can go onstage and give that's something. Man, that does me right in."

enjoyment to that many thousand people,

Keith holding court behind the bar at the Crown & Cushion hotel, Chipping Norton, with Ronnie Lane, Vivian Stanshall and Chris Welch.

JOHN MEARS

FORMER NEIGHBOUR, CHAUFFEUR AND FRIEND

"I used to live in Enfield, Middlesex and Keith bought a house opposite ours. This was late 1969. I only got to meet Keith because I went to investigate the sound of smashing bottles outside our house. It was winter and at the time it was snowing. Moonie was standing in the middle of the road, wearing only some leopard-skin underpants. His wife [Kim Kerrigan] was at the front door throwing beer bottles at him. They had clearly had a bit of a row and it didn't look like it was going to calm down. I invited him to come inside and at this point I still had no idea who he was. I gave him a dressing gown to wrap around himself and poured him a large brandy.

"When I say I didn't know who Keith was, it is true. I was a Beatles boy. I knew of The Who but I wasn't a fan as such. Over time Keith and I got to know each other. A few weeks after Keith moved in, his driver, friend and bodyguard Neil Boland died tragically. Keith actually came over to mine the night it happened and he was in a real mess. That whole incident really affected Keith. He became a recluse for a few weeks and wouldn't leave his house. 'Legs' Larry Smith came round to look after him quite a bit during that period. That tragic event stayed with Keith for a long time. I remember he used Mandrax a lot and on a few occasions I was called over by Kim to help Keith because he had taken too many. Sometimes he hadn't swallowed them properly and this made him froth at the mouth. I would have to try to get the pills out and keep him awake by walking him around.

"I don't know if this was just one of Keith's bizarre ways of trying to get some attention, but attention was something that he craved. Keith fed off people's reactions to what he was doing. He would do things like walk into a boozer, order a pint of lager and a large brandy, down the brandy but then pour the lager over his head.

"The reason he got a lilac Rolls-Royce was so that people would notice him. By this time I was working for Keith. This came about after he invited me to a party at his house; Ronnie Lane and 'Legs' Larry Smith were there that night. The party went on all night and in the morning Keith told me that he needed to get to Track Records because he had a meeting with them. I offered to drive him, he accepted and the next thing I knew he had offered me the job as his driver, replacing Neil. I accepted. The day after he took me on he told me that he didn't want the Bentley back, the one that had killed Neil. Instead he gave me three grand and told me to go and buy a Roller. I returned with a dark green Roller but he told me that he didn't like the colour. 'I want it sprayed lilac,' he said. In 1970 a car like that stuck out like a sore thumb.

"Keith also got to know my parents, whom I lived with. My dad's furniture business got sold and he was looking for something else to do and somehow the idea arose that it might be a good idea to buy a hotel with Keith. So they did; they bought the Crown & Cushion in Chipping Norton, Oxfordshire.

"And even though Keith owned the hotel he still occasionally smashed it up. The whole time Keith and my dad had the hotel, it was like a big party. There were some wild parties and one night Keith got so pissed he fell down the stairs and dislocated his collarbone. The thing was he was due to play

Top Of The Pops the following day. He did it but they tied a bit of string to his arm and moved him around like a puppet.

Keith and my dad kept the pub for about three years before they sold up. It just wasn't viable to hold onto. I mean Keith used to spend a lot of time there, but with all his mates and they would just have a big party. It didn't work as a hotel.

I was at the *Live At Leeds* show and the Isle of Wight. The Who played at a lot of universities at that time. People couldn't keep their eyes off Keith when he played. Before Keith I was a Ringo man but seeing the energy that Keith had was incredible. As soon as he walked on stage you could see the adrenalin kick in and he would just take off. Up until that point he could be as pissed as a fart, but as soon as he got behind that set of drums, he was a showman.

"Keith's death was a tremendous accident. It was tragic because at the time he was trying to stop himself drinking. The trouble with Keith was that when he took stuff [drugs] he took it all. When I first started working for him he would send me out to get his leapers [pills] and downers for him, and he would have to take loads of them. I mean he would start the day with a handful of uppers, then we'd go to the Speakeasy and he would have a drink and more pills, then we'd get back about five, he'd have some dinner, then he'd have some Mandrax to try and help him sleep. Then he would wake up the next day and do it all over again.

"After a while I stopped working for Keith because I got offered a job working for The Beatles. I was Ringo's driver and had met Ringo through Keith. I kept in contact with Keith and would see him around. I visited Tara a few times and saw him at Pinewood Studios during the time he was filming *200 Motels* with Zappa. It was sad to hear what happened to Keith but he was always going to live up to the song and 'die before he got old'."

Keith's lilac Rolls-Royce Silver Cloud and his Mercedes-Benz 300SEL 6.3 outside Peter 'Dougal' Butler's parents' house in Hayes.

JOHN SCHOLLAR

THE BEACHCOMBERS

The Beachcombers

"I grew up in an area not far from Wembley, where Keith grew up. Most of the early Beachcomber gigs were in venues in that area. We had a drummer, but he wasn't really up to scratch, so we kicked him out and auditioned a few drummers. Keith was one of them and he was just superb. He was also very young, I don't think even 16, but when he started playing we all looked at each other and knew he was something special.

For a little bloke he produced so much energy and noise. And he made the most of what kit he had. Even with us he rarely used a hi-hat.

"When The Beachcombers started out we were playing Shadows numbers and listening to Elvis, Buddy Holly and Eddie Cochran, and when the surf stuff came in we did some Beach Boys and Jan & Dean songs too. In fact people on the circuit knew us as the shadows of the Shadows. Can you imagine Keith playing drums on Shadows songs? He was shit-hot at it and would add a bit more drive to it. We had to drop some ballads because Keith would rock them up a bit too much. Plus he pranked

Fifteen-year-old Keith Moon, fresh out of school.

The Beachcombers unloading their equipment for a gig at Hastings Pier in the summer of 1963.

about. While playing 'Are You Lonesome Tonight' one night, Keith produced one of those duck decoy calls, the ones people blow when they go duck shooting, and in the middle of the verse he would blow it making the 'quack quack' sound. He even had a starting pistol one night and accidentally shot our singer.

"We had some laughs in The Beachcombers. There was a time when a friend managed to get hold of a pantomime horse, from the Wembley Ice Rink. He brought it to one of our shows and Keith loved it. He climbed inside it, fooled around, and we couldn't get him out. Keith held onto the pantomime horse's head and took it to some audition we had to do in central London. He spent most of that night inside it, charging around Piccadilly Circus. I remember we both went for a

wee in one of the public urinals in Leicester Square. Keith kept the horse's head on. God knows what people thought when they saw him. Another time he tried to get on one of the old London buses, the ones where you have to jump on the back. The conductor tried to refuse him but Keith just replied, 'It's okay we'll go upstairs and don't worry, the horse don't smoke.' The whole time Keith was in The Beachcombers it was non-stop laughter.

One of the things that doesn't really tend to come out in books about The Who or Keith is what a nice bloke he was and even back then he was. I was only talking to one of Keith's sisters at the weekend and we were saying that there were only a few people that really knew him and saw that side of him. Even when he was a huge rock star he would still ring me up and invite me to gigs; several times, in the early Who days, I ended up bringing Keith home in my car. And there was never a hint of 'how big I am'.

"I remember he was on *Top Of The Pops* one time and just after the show he rang me up and asked, 'So how was it, mate?' He did several things like that. In the early days there were times when he'd tell me about a gig and the next thing I knew I would be picking him up and taking him to it. It was only when The Who got much bigger did he become a bit distant and a bit wild.

"The Who were lovely blokes. I knew them when they were The Detours; we played the same clubs on the circuit. I was there on the night Keith got up and played drums with them. We all knew that Doug [Sandom] had left the band. I mean Keith wouldn't have done it otherwise. As soon as I heard Keith play with them I just knew that he had found the band that he should be in and they had found their drummer.

"I remember when The Who did a university tour. Keith rang me and said, 'John, we're playing in Brighton, do you want to come? Come over and we'll drive down in the Rolls'. I said I did and my girlfriend (now my wife) and me drove over to his

The Beachcombers, L–R: Tony Brind, Ron Chenery, Keith, John Schollar and Norman Mitchener.

place. But when I got there Keith had left a note on the door where he had scribbled some message about having to go and pick someone else up and see you in Brighton. The problem was, I didn't have a clue where he was playing in Brighton.

"We drove to Brighton and flagged someone down who told me The Who were playing in the Sussex University. So we drove there. We parked up and headed for the venue. We walked through the doors and walked up some steps but got stopped by the bouncers. I said, 'We are invited by Keith,' to which he replied, 'Yeah and plenty of others. No tickets. No entry.'

"Thankfully, a few minutes later Keith turned up, headed straight for us and gave my missus a big hug. I then told him that we were having trouble getting in. 'Right' he says, and goes and demands that the manager comes and speaks with him. The manager appeared and Keith explained that he had invited some friends down from London and the bouncers wouldn't let them in, but there was still a no ticket, no entry type attitude. 'Hmm,' says Keith, 'Have you ever seen The Who play without a drummer? I tell you they are bloody awful.'

"By this time there's a reasonable sized group that had gathered around us, all listening to what was going on. The manager seeing this eventually gives in and says it's okay for Keith's friends to go

Keith onstage with The Beachcombers in 1963.

inside. To this Keith turns to the crowd and shouts out 'the manager says that any of my friends that don't have tickets can go in. Who doesn't have tickets?' To which about a dozen hands go up in the air. We all got in and that was what Keith was like.

"The missus and I followed Keith into the dressing room and there were John and Pete sitting around a little table with a bottle of brandy. They filled up small plastic beakers and handed us drinks and we chatted. They were also being interviewed by some journalist and as soon as Keith got involved it just turned into *The Goon Show*. It was very funny to watch.

"There was a bit of time before the show so we decided to go to the bar to get a drink. When we got there the barman says, 'Oh Mr Moon, these

people have been waiting for you to arrive because they want you to open a tab, so that they can have a drink.'

"'Oh okay', says Keith, get them a drink. But I stepped in and said. 'Sod them Keith, just have a drink with me', and I ordered some brandies. The barman said 'but what about them?' pointing to the crowd. Keith looks at them then at me and replies, 'My friend says sod them, they can wait.'

After a drink Keith had to leave us and go and do the show but before he left he told us that he had arranged for us to sit in one of the balcony booths. We sat down and the waiter appeared with a tray full of drinks for us. Keith had arranged that too. Keith could be incredibly thoughtful and generous. He was a great friend.

"I was mortified when I heard that Keith had died. Unfortunately, I heard about it on the news. I came in, sat down, turned on the TV and the news about Keith was on the telly. I just couldn't believe it. Then the phone started ringing and people were asking me if I had seen the news. I was so upset. And then I had to ring Keith's mum, Kitty. We spoke and she was so upset. We even talked about the funeral and she said she wanted a private event and didn't want it turning into a circus.

"The funeral was held at Golders Green Crematorium and was an actually brilliant but sad day out. Every major rock star was there and after the service they were all sitting around telling stories about Keith, it was amazing. In fact the table that I was sitting on was getting louder and louder and Kitty came over. I looked at her and said, 'Oh sorry Kit' but she said, 'No John, you're telling stories aren't you, you carry on, that's what Keith would have wanted.'

"I remember looking around the room and seeing Charlie Watts laughing and Pete Townshend in a hell of state. It was obvious that everybody loved Keith, even though he had done so many things to also piss people off.

"There were loads of flowers too. Roger had sent a large bunch fashioned into a floral television set with a smashed champagne bottle hanging out of it. I spent some time reading the labels attached to the flowers and there were so many from famous people like Eric Clapton and members of The Rolling Stones. There was also a small posy of flowers and I looked to see who they were from. It turned out to be from a children's home that Keith had helped out at some point.

"After the service Kit asked me (and two members of The Beachcombers, Tony and Norman) to go back to the house. The house was jam packed with people, you couldn't move, so Kit said to us, 'You boys go out into the garden for a bit of privacy.' We went to the garden and found Roger, Pete and John standing there. There was complete silence. It was very sad.

"The other sad thing was that people were expecting something to happen to Keith. I thought he'd end up having an accident in a car. I think we just sensed that he was never going to make old age. At first the media tried to make out that Keith had committed suicide but that was nonsense. Kit even said to me: 'I don't know what this suicide business is all about.' I replied: 'No Kit, it's rubbish, he was too much of a coward to do anything like that. He couldn't stand any pain. Anyway, if Keith was going to do anything like that he would have hired Wembley Stadium and blown himself up in a coffin or something.'

"A few days after the funeral Kit phoned me and told me that someone had rung her to tell her that lots of Keith's stuff was in a room over in Shepperton Studios. She asked me to go over and have a look to see what was there. There was loads of stuff just lying around and anyone could have walked in and walked off with anything, and quite possibly some people did. But I phoned Kit and told her that she needed to get Keith's stuff out and store it somewhere safer.

"Kit went over and collected the stuff. There were gold discs and all sorts. Kit then rang me and asked me to pop in and see her after work one day. So I went over to her place and she had piles of gold discs and awards scattered around her living room. It was an amazing sight and she told me to just pick whatever I wanted. There was some very rare stuff and I explained to Kit that she had some priceless stuff and should hold onto it. But she wanted me to have something so I took one of the gold discs for *Tommy* which I have on my wall to this day."

TONY BARBADOS

DRUMMER, MOD, ACTOR

"Keith Moon deserves to be called a legend. I grew up in a household where music from bands like The Kinks, Stones, Beatles and Who was always around. Then when I was about eight years old I saw Keith Moon playing with The Who on the television and from then I knew I wanted to play drums.

"By the time I was in my teens I was playing drums and the Mod revival thing was happening. I was listening to bands like The Jam and Secret Affair. Soon after Moon died The Jam released a version of 'So Sad About Us' on the B-side to their 'Down In The Tube Station At Midnight' single and it had an image of Keith's face on the back cover. This was The Jam's way of acknowledging what a

great man Keith Moon was. I thought it was a great thing to do and Rick Buckler did a sterling job on it and played it his own way. On hearing the news Clem Burke of Blondie kicked over his drum kit on the stage at Glastonbury; Clem was a massive Moon fan.

"It was because of bands like The Jam, Secret Affair and Squire that I then went back and investigated bands like The Who in more detail. And out of all those bands around in the sixties The Who seemed to have something different. Bands like The Kinks and Small Faces were like gangs, all aiming in one direction towards a certain goal, whereas I think The Who were still a gang, but a gang of individuals who all brought something amazing and incredible to the band. It all came together like some sort of magic potion.

"The *Quadrophenia* film was big for me, but I already had the album. When I first got into The Who I was given a load of records by some people that I worked with, who had been Mods back in the sixties. The *Quadrophenia* album with its black-and-white cover was among them. The film sort of brought to life the songs and the characters included inside the album sleeve.

"I always go back to the *Quadrophenia* album and I think it's my favourite album for Keith Moon's drumming. People say that everyone's got a book inside them or, if you're a band, an album. I think for The Who and for Keith it was *Quadrophenia*. The drums sound great and his playing is superb; he pretty much follows Daltrey's vocals throughout the whole album.

"It certainly doesn't surprise me that there's still so much interest in Keith Moon so many years after his death. Anyone that starts to learn to play the drums finds their way to Keith Moon."

The back cover of The Jam's single 'Down In The Tube Station At Midnight' with the photo of Keith Moon.

CHARLIE MOON FOX

DRUMMER AND KEITH MOON'S NEPHEW

"It's because Keith was my uncle that I now play drums. When I was growing up I was around all the stuff to do with my uncle; my mum, Lesley, is one of Keith's sisters. Plus I was always going to my nan's house and seeing pictures and film footage of him playing the drums. No other instrument grabbed me like the drums and it came quite naturally.

"I think it was when I was around 14 years old that I properly realised who my uncle was. I started going to some of The Who conventions and it kinda hit home that Keith was a big deal. I feel hugely proud of him and all the smashing up of his gear was brilliant too. He was special and I like the way that he played his drums in such a free manner; he just seemed to play whatever he wanted to and I think he paved the way for others to follow. My uncle certainly inspired me and I improvise a lot when I'm playing. How he played helped me discover my own style. Keith's playing was fluid and unique and lots of people have drawn influences from him.

"I have some bits that belonged to Keith. I have one of his 24 inch Zildjian ride cymbals; it's an absolute monster and I must admit that I sometimes use it when I play live. I also have one of the floor toms from the Spirit Of Lily kit and a couple of drum sticks that I keep safe, but have used on occasion when I can't find any sticks, then I realise what I'm doing and put them back."

Left: Keith on set at Rediffusion's Ready Steady Go!, *Friday 3 December 1965–the day of release of the* My Generation *album.*

CHRIS CHARLESWORTH

FORMER MELODY MAKER *WRITER AND* 'JUST BACKDATED' *BLOGGER*

"It was in Dunstable in 1970 that I first saw The Who after having recently joined **Melody Maker**. I was already a huge fan of the band, but this was the first concert that I had been to seen them as a reviewer. They were doing *Tommy* and it was a magic show; I had a brilliant view and watched from a good place and went back to *Melody Maker* and wrote a good review.

"And then about a week later the phone rang and it was Keith Moon. 'Hello, is that Chris? This is Keith Moon of The Who,' he said. I was absolutely staggered. 'I just want to thank you for that great review that you gave the band,' he continued. I said thank you and added that The Who were my favourite band, to which he responded, 'Thank you, yes, they're my favourite band too.' He signed off the conversation by telling me that we should have a drink together in the Speakeasy some night, then said, 'Good night, dear boy.'

"I put the phone down and felt quite blown away. I mean I didn't expect that at all. During my time as a music journalist I reviewed plenty of bands and none of the others ever phoned me up to thank me and here was Keith Moon of The Who doing just that; and they certainly didn't need any good reviews written about them by then, as they were massive.

"Then one night down at the Speakeasy I saw Keith and I went over and introduced myself, and we had that drink together. At the end of the night he told me that The Who would be playing at the Hammersmith Palais in London in October [1970] and that I should be his guest. We arranged a

meeting place and I was his guest for the night. And it was that night that I met the other members of The Who. After the concert we went out to a club and had dinner, and from that night on we became friends.

"I had a childhood friend who lived near Chertsey and I would often go and spend weekends there. Keith found out and invited me to his home, Tara House. So I sometimes went and hung out with Keith and spent nights having drinking sessions in his local pub. I ended up having to crash at his place a few times. Once I drove him over to Englefield Green to a pub called The Fox & Hounds, where I knew the landlord – only time I've ever driven a Roller. A lot of the time he was out of his brain but he was great company with it. He was very, very funny and I found him to be incredibly generous; he would never let me pay for a drink. And because he was like this everyone assumed that he was very rich, but because he was such a big spender, he just wasn't.

"From this period on I went to see The Who lots of times and Keith was always very friendly. I wasn't the only journalist that he befriended; he had a habit of making friends with journalists from other music papers like the *NME* too. Because I got close to The Who I spent many concerts watching them from the side of the stage and observing Keith from those positions was a mind-boggling experience. I used to try and position myself on John's side of the stage because it was always much calmer than Pete's side. I would watch Keith, this whole bundle of energy, and think how does he do that? There was no one else like him.

"I was in the fortunate position of being invited to go on the road with The Who in America. It was a brilliant way to earn a living. When he went to live

Chris Charlesworth and friend with Keith and Annette Walter-Lax at the launch party for the Tommy *movie, New York City, 18 March 1975.*

in America we sort of lost touch a bit; but we still did see each other from time to time, when I was also in California. I have written about some of my experiences and relationship with Keith quite extensively in my blog 'Just Backdated'.

"The last time that I saw Keith was at a party being held for Lynyrd Skynyrd in New York and that was in 1976. He was looking a bit rough and a bit overweight. That was the night that I learned he was having money troubles and wasn't as rich as people thought. But all this aside, it doesn't

surprise me that there is still so much interest in Keith Moon to this day. He was such an iconic figure and will always come out on top of the list of the most hedonistic rock stars, but this was just part of Keith's life – he was a great drummer and he played with great feeling. Yes, at times he could be a bit sloppy, but he was so original and could be very spontaneous. I feel very fortunate to have been able to see Keith play so many times. And Keith certainly loved being a rock star."

"I'm the greatest Keith Moon-type drummer in

the world!"

DARRIN MOONEY

PRIMAL SCREAM

"*When I think of Keith Moon I do think madness, but I also think a great drum feel; he had loads of energy.* And it's that sort of energy that I think is lacking in many drummers today. I think modern music misses people like Keith Moon.

"Moon's drumming style was raw: pure and raw. My favourite Who album is *Who's Next* and there are parts of his drumming on that that are so tight and then some of it is so fucking trashy and brilliant. His drumming was just perfect. It wasn't too clean and it wasn't too dirty, just perfect.

"I first discovered Keith Moon's drumming when I was about five years old; my dad had records from bands like The Who and Led Zep and he played *Who's Next* a lot. I can remember him blasting the album out and thinking to myself 'I wanna be a drummer.' When I hear 'Baba O'Riley' I just want to hit toms and when I've hit them toms I want to get more toms and hit them too.

I took a lot of inspiration from Moon's style of drumming and tried to put that into my own drumming style, especially the way he did his big fills. Only when he did it, it would be like woooh! Moon also had musicality and not all drummers have that.

"He was able to accent in a brilliant way and it wasn't always over-complicated, but he did it in a unique way. I loved the way he would just put a fill in anywhere in the bar and anywhere in the song. It's unusual. Keith Moon wasn't like a jazz drummer, he wasn't like a technical drummer; he played with all the accents that he heard and played what he felt. It was as if his limbs had a mind of their own and he just went with it.

"It was as if Moon had a punk attitude to playing and played the way he wanted, and didn't give a fuck if people didn't want it because he was going to do it any way. In the music business, maybe more today, most drummers are always being told what to play by whoever's in charge. I'm sure Keith wouldn't have put up with someone telling him to play this tom here or that tom there. I think he would have told them to fuck off.

"Nowadays when I think about the lunatic side of Keith's life, sometimes I think it's hilarious and other times I think it's quite sad. I think the same about all those guys, Hendrix and Bonham; they all went far too young. It would have been interesting to hear them speak about those days if they'd got older and were able to look back. Part of the problem for Keith was that he grew a reputation early on for being the loon and once he had that protection around him and knew he could smash a Rolls Royce up and not go to prison, I can see it would be easy to do it.

"I don't believe The Who could have been The Who without Keith. Keith was a big voice in the band and Keith wasn't one of those band members that people hadn't heard of. This is the same for a lot of bands though; The Jam wouldn't have been The Jam if they hadn't had Rick Buckler."

Left: Keith with The Who at the 6th National Jazz and Blues Festival, Windsor, Berkshire, 30 July 1966. At the end of their 40-minute set Pete Townshend destroyed his guitar and amps, Roger Daltrey threw his microphone and Keith demolished this drum kit. All the while, Chris Stamp and Kit Lambert stood in the wings, throwing smoke bombs onto the stage.

The Who on Rediffusion TV's Ready Steady Go! *in 1965, broadcast on Friday evenings.*

PHIL GOULD

LEVEL 42

LEVEL 42

"I had an older brother who listened to a lot of music and through his music I discovered the drummers like Keith Moon and Ringo Starr. I loved 'Join Together' and thought the intro was very cool. I remember the first time I tried to copy Moon's drumming on that intro. I just couldn't get it because I didn't understand what the 'drag' was. I just couldn't see how he created that sound using his left hand.

"Listening to 'Join Together' also helped to show me that not only was Keith Moon a fantastic drummer but he was a great musician too; and the older I got and more experienced at playing the drums I got the more I understood this to be the case. I saw Keith Moon as being very musical. You can watch footage of him and he is often sitting behind his kit singing along with the record and copying the melody with his drumming.

"I saw The Who when they played one of their concerts at the Charlton football ground. This was 1976 and to be fair he was a bit rusty, but I've seen footage of the concert since and you can see he really plays along to the melodies. You can hear the interaction between him and Daltrey and you can also see how he punches out some of the pushes coming from Townshend's guitar. I don't think Moon gets as much credit as he should for being able to do that sort of stuff.

"There were times when Moon didn't even play

Right: The 1973 film That'll Be The Day, *starring David Essex and Ringo Starr. Keith played the character JD Clover, the drummer in Stormy Tempest's (Billy Fury) backing group The Typhoons.*

with a hi-hat; he just didn't even bother to include it in the kit. You watch footage of him on something like *Ready Steady Go!* and he has a hi-hat then he stops using one, which is sort of odd. Then he returns to using hi-hats on something like 'Who Are You'.

"When I was younger I lived on the Isle of Wight. Some scenes from the film *That'll Be The Day* were filmed there and of course Keith was in the film. In fact some of the scenes were shot in the school that I went to. During the filming some event was held on the end of Shanklin pier and my brother was involved because he was a deejay.

Nat Cohen presents an Anglo EMI Film
Goodtimes Enterprises production

That'll Be The Day

starring
**DAVID ESSEX
ROSEMARY
LEACH
RINGO STARR**

guest stars
**JAMES   BILLY
BOOTH   FURY
KEITH MOON**

Executive Producer ROY BAIRD
Directed by **CLAUDE WHATHAM**
Original story and screenplay by
RAY CONNOLLY
Produced by **DAVID PUTTNAM**
and **SANFORD LIEBERSON**
Technicolor ®
Distributed by Anglo **EMI** Film Distributors Limited

EMI

Leading with two bass drums: Keith, on his Pictures of Lily kit, with Pete Townshend on the 1967 US tour supporting Herman's Hermits.

He asked me to take my new (which was actually an old Premier Olympic silver sparkle) drum kit along. I had only owned the drum kit for a few weeks. I don't know why but Keith Moon appeared and wanted to have a play on the kit. The deejay played some Who records and Keith Moon played along to them. He bashed the hell out of my poor little old drum kit. So I stood watching the drummer from The Who beating the shit out of my drum kit and he was killing it. At this stage in my drumming career (I was only 15) I didn't even know that people played the drums like that. Moon hit my drums so hard, I actually thought he was hitting them so hard because he purposefully wanted to destroy my kit.

"If I had known better I should have said something and who knows, maybe he would have had his people send me a brand new massive Premier drum kit. But instead I mentioned it to Moon's minder and he gave me a pound coin. When I told my mum what had happened and showed her the kit she was furious and I was the one that got into trouble.

"There was something about The Who that was actually jaw-dropping and Keith Moon contributed to that. It's as if it was something that shouldn't have worked but it did. I think a lot of other bands would have fallen apart much quicker if they had had someone like Keith Moon in them. But instead The Who have had a huge impact and generated so much power, it's really quite extraordinary.

"I grew up listening to a lot of funk drummers and they tend to lead with their hi-hats and snares and the bass sits behind, but one of the things about Keith Moon was that he was one of the first drummers to lead with his bass drum. Maybe Moon was inspired by Phil Seamen because he was one of the earliest drummers to make the bass drum sound large. Moon also made his drums sound louder than a lot of his peers. If you listen to a Kinks record beside a Who record The Kinks' drum sound is much quieter, so I think Keith Moon helped push rock drumming to the front. I think this is just one of the reasons that made Moon such an influential drummer and he really did come out with some impressive bass drum patterns.

"Keith Moon played with a great deal of drive and energy but he also played with a great deal of feel too. I think a lot of this type of stuff gets lost because people focus on what they think is just thrashing around, but it wasn't. I think in many ways Moon is overrated for the wrong reasons and underrated for the right. Keith Moon was both a great drummer and a great musician."

IAN McNABB

ICICLE WORKS / RINGO STARR & HIS ALL-STAR BAND / CRAZY HORSE

"The way that history has treated Keith is that he was a lunatic and a mad man and nothing more than a crazy rock star who drove Rolls Royces into swimming pools. I think this is unfortunate really. I agree, he seems to have been a bit mad, but he seemed to be a nice guy with it too. I never met Keith but people that I know that met him have said he was a sweet guy.

"There was just nobody like Keith Moon, the way he played the drums. He was a frontman all the while rattling around the tom-toms. When you listen to Keith's drumming it's just absolutely astounding. People have tried to copy him but like Keith said, 'I'm the best Keith Moon-type drummer in the world'.

"When Keith played he played melodic drums and played along with Townshend. I've heard that John Entwistle had to watch Keith's feet as he played the bass drums. The Who as a band were very unusual, they had great songs and great musicians, but it was as if Townshend was the drummer: he kept the time, which allowed Keith to do lots of unusual stuff. It's remarkable to hear how Keith follows Townshend's guitar. Keith Moon just suited what The Who were. I think Noel Gallagher once said of The Who that everyone in the band is playing a solo all at the same time.

'My Generation' is just outrageous; the ending to that song is like a nuclear explosion. But one of my favourite albums and one that doesn't seem to get spoken about so often is *The Who By Numbers*. Keith's drumming on the first track 'Slip Kid' is just unbelievable. It's a song that Keith has obviously thought out and he'd got the cowbell going, and if you listen to that it reminds you that no other drummer has ever sounded like Keith Moon. I mean a drummer like John Bonham was power and groove and Ginger Baker was a jazzer but Keith was on his own.

"It must have just been incredible to have been in a band with Keith Moon. So much was different and new. He rarely used a drum riser, he wanted to be down among the amps and mix with the band. Yes, he had an ego and he was a performer and show-off but it worked for The Who.

"There's a story that Buddy Rich went to see The Who play on the *Quadrophenia* tour. Rich sat behind Keith throughout the show and watched him. When Keith came off stage he went up to Buddy Rich and asked him what he thought. Buddy Rich replied: 'Are you getting paid a lot of money for playing like that?' 'A fortune,' Keith replies, to which Buddy returns, 'Well you just keep on playing like that then'.

"Over the years I've been asked a lot who my heroes are and I have often said, 'Keith Moon – but I wouldn't want him in my band'. I mean I have a couple of songs that he would shine on but I'm the one at the front and I'm the one trying to sing a song."

Right: Two bass drums, kettle drums and more . . . The USA & Canada Fall tour, 1976.

"I'm listening to what Pete's doing; I'm listening to what I'm doing. A drummer doesn't need to think

what John's doing. I don't have time to think about about what he's doing. He just does it."

Roger, Keith, Pete and John in Paris for the Ready Steady Go! *gig at La Locomotive club, April 1966.*

JIM McCARTY

THE YARDBIRDS

"An absolutely mad bloke but an absolutely brilliant drummer. The Yardbirds and The Who played together a few times but I especially remember a *Ready Steady Go!* programme that we both did, that was filmed in Paris. I think this may have been The Who's first European appearance. We were at La Locomotive club. I can't recall why, but I needed to use Keith's drums that night. I sat on the drum stool and thought 'What on earth is going on here?' because there was blood all over the drum skins. I presumed that he had played so hard he had made his hands bleed. I don't know why I was surprised because just before I went on to play we had a brief chat and he told me that he'd dropped a handful of leapers [pills].

"After the show I popped outside and I could see The Who surrounded by photographers and TV cameramen and so forth, then they disappeared down a side alley, stood in a row and all had a piss up against the wall. I don't know if the TV cameras caught that or not.

"Keith did an amazing drum solo the first night I saw The Who at the Marquee and what struck me was just how powerful a player he was. Keith played like no other drummer at that time. Other drummers like myself and Charlie Watts came up through the jazz route but Keith didn't: he was a full-on rock drummer, he was an incredible power-house. He seemed to be able to hit lots of things at the same time and I couldn't work out how he was doing it.

"There really was no other drummer like Keith Moon before him. Drummers like Charlie [Watts] and I were much cooler but Keith just went for it; it was almost like he played a lead part rather than just sitting back a bit, like most drummers did in the mid-sixties. Maybe he deliberately filled the space that a rhythm guitar would have filled.

"Keith was a great guy and a good laugh to be around. Sometimes he would pop in to see us play. I would also see him around the clubs, like the Speakeasy and the Cromwellian. He was always out and about a lot.

"It was a shock when I heard the news of Keith's death. It was a horrible time around that seventies period because there was more and more of those sort of deaths happening, what with Jim Morrison, Mama Cass and Jimi Hendrix. They were casualties of a certain lifestyle. And there were plenty of stories going around about Keith's crazy lifestyle, stories like piranhas in the bath and so on, but those things weren't important to the people that knew him. Those that knew him will remember him as a very reasonable guy, very nice, always willing to have a chat and a good laugh to be around.

"Sometimes people ask me who I think was the best drummer and I always say Keith Moon and Ginger Baker. Whenever I saw Keith play I watched him very closely and he was a great drummer, and he certainly influenced how I played."

JOHN COGHLAN

STATUS QUO

SQ

"*Showman is what initially comes to mind.* I can remember one time that I met Keith. Status Quo were recording at some studio in London and Keith showed up. I was introduced to him and I tell you what, man, he was as quiet as a mouse, which I thought was strange because I expected some outrageous guy. I realised that Keith wasn't 'that' person all the time and, if anything, was 'that' person much of the time because he felt that he needed to be in front of people. Keith was great and I think he was expected to have to throw stuff out of hotel windows. We never did that though because we didn't want to have to pay for it.

"I think Keith was a much greater drummer than what people saw and gave him credit for. He grew up listening to the same drummers as us from that period, but he played different. John Bonham was the same and we also miss him. There was no one like Keith before Keith; he was the only one really out there. The nearest was Sandy Nelson, in the way of playing leading drums. I mean when people went to watch The Who I bet they didn't watch Pete Townshend's arm swinging around, I bet they were watching Keith.

"The excesses of rock'n'roll can be very hard. I was doing it for 20 years and in the end I had enough and just said 'fuck this' and got on the plane and flew home. That lifestyle can get you down. And once you've done it all–and I don't just mean the drugs, I mean been there, played that, stayed up all night and so on–you can start to think... well, what the fuck's left? I took a year off playing drums before I returned to it again and you soon find out who your friends really are. I'm sure Keith would have felt all these things at various times."

Right: Keith, the perfect gentleman–even when putting on his socks.

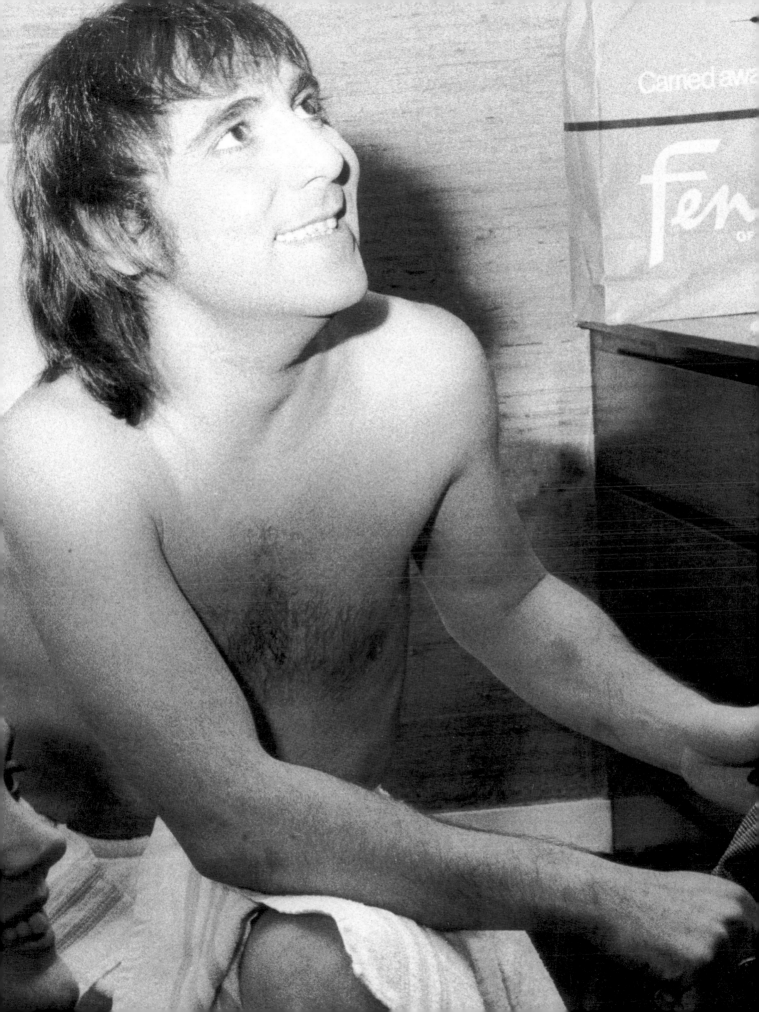

Keith with The Who during the 1973 Quadrophenia *tour of the US.*

MAX WEINBERG

BRUCE SPRINGSTEEN'S E STREET BAND

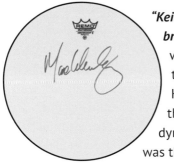

"Keith Moon was a ground-breaking drummer. He was as influential in the sixties as Gene Krupa was in the thirties. Moon was very dynamic and in my view was the lead instrument in The Who, which is an unusual situation. Pete Townshend's part was very much built around playing rhythm, and the way this worked with Keith's drumming gave the band a really exciting and dynamic and explosive sound. The way the four members came together really did provide the template for a true rock band.

"I'm sure Keith Moon played his drums the way he did as a reaction to Pete Townshend's song writing. In many ways Pete was like Duke Ellington; he wrote his music for the talents of the people in his band. And I think Pete understood Keith's style and so wasn't going to write songs for a guy that was only going to keep a steady beat. Over my years of recording with Bruce my drumming has been very specific for his songs. I kinda feel that I provide the background landscape for which the action then takes place. And I have had my moments of playing pretty wild on some of those recordings. And that's partly because I was just one of many drummers from a generation that was influenced by Keith Moon's drumming with The Who.

"When I started out playing drums I listened to drummers of any stripe. I listened to the drummers that played jazz, rock and Dixieland; and back in those days you had to be a generalist and be able to play many styles. But back in the sixties I was part of the rock generation and so I wanted to play rock music. And I was privileged to see The Who's first US concert, which was in April 1967 in New York City. It was the 'Murray the K' show that also included Cream and Wilson Pickett. I was 16 years old and went along with my girlfriend of the time. We somehow managed to get seats in the fifth row. Up until this point I had heard 'I Can't Explain' but I hadn't even seen a clip of the band. But being that close to The Who and watching Keith just blew me away. Being that close too meant that I could really feel the intensity. I had never seen anything like it. Keith Moon was like a human dynamo.

The Who's first venture into the US, on the 'Murray the K' show along with 'The' Cream.

"That show Keith was an unbelievable drummer and really technical drummer too. He was a freak of nature. He was a total original, he played with incredible finesse and speed, and he had incredible ideas too. I walked away thinking the band defined rock music and how a rock band should be. I was also both impressed and confused about the way he trashed that beautiful red drum set. I mean I watched him kick his drums all over the stage and that wasn't my style at all.

"When I was recording *The River* album with Bruce Springsteen in the late seventies I was listening to a lot of Keith Moon drumming at that time. I remember that Bruce's songs really led me to discover The Who all over again. But it still amazes me that those Who songs just don't get old. 'I Can See For Miles' still sounds as good to me today as it did when I first heard it back in Junior High School. I played that song so much that I learned it note for note. It's been indelibly imprinted in my mind. The drumming on that song is perfect.

"Other than playing the drums, the other thing that Keith and I had was that he was also a huge Beach Boys fan. They were my favourite band; I grew up listening, and loving surf music. And Keith loved to play Beach Boys' songs but he didn't play anything like the drums on those records. He played his own style. He probably ruined a lot of drummers because they wanted to play like him but couldn't. He became the world's greatest rock drummer and he completely invented his own style, and no one else could play like that.

"Keith Moon had everything you want in a drummer. There was excitement, chops, imagination and execution. He was special and unique, and if you take everything else away he was a great drummer. Another example would be Frank Sinatra. I mean if you take away all the other crazy stuff out of his life, except his singing, then you are left with the essence of Frank Sinatra. The same can be applied to Keith Moon too. If you take away all the Rolls Royces in the pool and being the model for the *Spinal Tap* exploding drummer and being an influence on literally everyone that came after him, you're left with the essence of Keith Moon as a drummer.

"One of my big thrills was playing at the Rock'n'roll Hall of Fame dinner the year The Who got inducted. At the end there was this big jam and somehow I got put on the drums and Pete, John and Roger joined me and a bunch of other people on the stage too. I got to play 'Pinball Wizard' with The Who.

"There's a newspaper in New York called *Village Voice* and in the music ad section there'd always be someone asking for a drummer who is influenced by Keith Moon, and this is 30 years after Keith Moon tragically passed away. When I see those ads I'm reminded that Keith Moon really did make a huge impact."

Keith with The Who during the 1973 Quadrophenia *tour of the US.*

DEBBI PETERSON

THE BANGLES

"What's the first thing that springs to mind?... a complete maniac but an amazing drummer.

I kinda became aware of The Who and Keith Moon in the late sixties. Tommy was a very influential record for me because there are some incredible drum parts on it. Tommy was a big deal for me and my friends. My older sister had a copy and would play it a lot and then I got a copy and would spend a lot of time listening to it with my friend and sometimes my brother, who was also a drummer and big Keith Moon fan.

Tommy was the record that spurred me on to want to know more about Keith Moon. I also saw some clips of The Who playing in the early days and watching Keith going wild on the drum set and knocking drums over was really something. I thought wow, imagine having the freedom to be like that, not care and just completely let go.

"When Keith played his drums, it was like they were an extension of him. He had such a unique style that was like complete abandonment. There seemed to be no set drum part and he would come up with something completely different in every section of the song. There was such variety in his playing. He was what I would describe as an unexpected drummer. I play drums in a more traditional way. I sing while I play, so I guess I keep it a little more controlled. Keith was nothing like that. When Keith played it sounded like he was out of control, but whatever he did worked for the songs. Keith definitely had a crazy way of making his drumming work fit with Townshend and Entwistle. I mean Pete played with such aggression and angst and this seemed to work and fuel Keith's drumming. The Who was like four very different individuals coming together and somehow making it work brilliantly, together.

"Yeah, I think a lot of Keith Moon's drumming skills get overshadowed by the lunacy stuff. The media focused so much on him doing crazy things that they failed to focus on his actual drumming talent, and that is a shame. Sure, he did have that reckless abandonment side, that was his way and I have spoken to lots of people that knew him and they say 'Yeah, that's how Keith was', but I don't think he gets enough respect for his actual drumming."

Left: The Who create some mayhem at the Piper Club in Rome, Italy, Sunday 26 February 1966.

NEVILLE CHESTERS

ONE OF THE WHO'S EARLY ROADIES

"Before I started working for The Who I was with The Merseybeats. I worked with them while they went to the top and then on their way down Kit Lambert spotted them. He decided that he wanted Billy Kinsley and Tony Crane as a singing duo and not as part of the band. Lambert then signed them as The Merseys and pulled in a different backing band. This was how I got to meet Kit and one night we went to see The Who play in West London. I thought they were really interesting and asked Kit if I could work with them as their roadie.

"At first he said I couldn't because they already had a roadie [Dave Langston]. But there was some

issue about the risks of the band's van being pinched and having all their equipment stolen. The van would often be parked up outside Dave's house every night. Someone had an idea to get a guard dog and Dave went down to the Battersea Dogs Home to get one, but while he was in the home someone stole the van, and as a result that was the end of Dave and I got the job. This was late 1964.

"Back in the early sixties I wanted to be a drummer, but when I looked at all the brilliant drummers playing around Liverpool, I thought I couldn't be as good as them so I didn't start. But with every band that I have worked with, I always follow the drummers. My first impression of Keith was that he was a drummer that just flailed, but then I saw so much more. I would watch him and think how could he do that; logically, it shouldn't work, but actually what he was doing was perfect. Keith wouldn't do anything straight like most drummers do. What he seemed to do was pack out a song with a mass of drum fills. He was extraordinarily amazing.

"When you watched Keith playing, it was like watching a great big spinning wheel. What you got from Keith was a continuous noise. Over the years I have seen, befriended and been taught some bits by various drummers (after The Who I went on the road with Cream and spent time with Ginger Baker) but there's nobody like Keith Moon. When it comes to drumming originality Keith Moon was to drums what Jimi Hendrix was to guitars. There really was only one Keith Moon.

"Out of the four members of The Who I was friendlier with John, but there were times when I

Above: The Merseybeats–Johnny Gustafson, Tony Crane, Aaron Williams and John Banks. Gustafson replaced Billy Kinsley in 1964.

Right: Keith tries his hand at the Hohner Melodica Piano 27 during The Who's tour of Germany, April 1967.

John, Keith and Kim hanging out on the set of Ready Steady Go!, *1966.*

couldn't hang out with John because he was always hanging out with Keith, and I would try to avoid hanging out with Keith because wherever he went he left a trail of destruction, which I found hard to be around. I mean I had enough of it having to put back together parts of his destroyed drum kits on the stage and he was very skilled at ruining a drum kit in three minutes. The thing was, Keith really only had a small-knit group of friends and they were all pretty much 'off the mark' types of guys.

"But as much as Keith did lunatic and seemingly uncontrollable things, in the studio he could pull it all together. Even though he would do a lot of fooling around, when it came down to it, he did get the work done. He was still quite unconventional though. But then he was unconventional in everything that he did. He was a powerhouse that made things work. I was with The Who when they made their first album *My Generation* and got to witness Keith in the studio. I actually also do a voiceover on a track off of the *A Quick One* album called 'I Need You'. There were three speaking parts that include me, Keith Moon and Chris Stamp.

"When I found out that Keith had died, it felt a bit like when I found out that Jimi [Hendrix] had died. It wasn't that much of a shock because I had sort of been expecting it for some time. If anything, I wondered how Keith managed to stay alive for so long. It was sad that most people seemed entertained by his mania, but there are a lot of people that see him for the great drummer that he was too."

EDDIE PHILLIPS

THE CREATION

"A great drummer that always tried to give 200%. I first met Keith because I was playing in the Mark Four at the time. Bill Fowler, our roadie, came to pick me up for a gig. He told me about The High Numbers... his words were: "There is a band in West London doing your act". It was to me one of those moments that stick in your memory, and he raved about the drummer, so that's when I first heard about Keith.

"I like drummers that keep it simple, just lay down the beat–Jack Jones was great at that, so I would not normally like Keith's style, but he could be busy and with great timing and still keep it rocking. I think Keith and John Entwistle were one of the great drum/bass combinations in rock history, their contribution was massive. I remember the first time the Mark Four played with The Who. It was in a dance hall over the top of Burtons the tailors in Uxbridge, and of course Keith gave it everything he had but offstage he was a different kind of bloke. We had a chat, I can't remember what about but he was a pretty cool chap. He was a great talent and it's very sad he went before his time."

AL MURRAY

COMEDIAN

"Keith Moon is all about how drumming used to be. He is the purest expression of what rock drumming used to be like. The funny thing is that he just wouldn't get hired now, there would be someone saying 'You can't do that.' I mean there were moments when he would play in time, he would drive the band by speeding up and slowing down and he played dramatically—he did all the things modern drummers are discouraged from doing. And yet Keith Moon is the archetypal rock drummer.

"There are some examples of Keith's drum tracks on YouTube, they're isolated drum tracks, and there's one from 'Won't Get Fooled Again'. When you listen to it, it sounds like he is playing out of time, but when you play the whole recording, what he does is right, he makes the whole song swing.

"Keith's drumming has such drama in it. His phrasing was that good—who cares if he played in time or not? And on 'Won't Get Fooled Again' there's other instruments playing in perfect time, but what Keith is doing is pure genius.

"Recording techniques have changed a lot since Keith's day, and he played his kit as one instrument. The way drums are recorded these days just wouldn't capture the sound and feel of the way Keith played.

"I also think Keith was more of a live drummer. When you watch any footage of his live performances his drumming takes on a whole different meaning and there's a whole new dimension. The Who were a great singles band, but live they were a band on a whole different level. It's almost as if there were two Whos really. There was the more controlled and polite band that went in the studio and recorded the singles and albums and then there was the band that performed on that massive stage on the Isle of Wight in 1969. They created a live vibe like no other band could achieve and I think that was down to Keith Moon. Keith's personality came through his playing and to some extent I think the Rolls Royce stories overshadowed so much more about Keith.

"The way I come at it, as a comic, is that Keith Moon had great timing, and I don't mean drumming timing. What Keith had was amazing timing. It's like comic timing, where he is breathing right with the music, the song and what everyone else is doing around him. I mean as though he is a noisy bugger but he was also listening to what the others were doing and what the song was doing.

"Keith's drumming style was this: take it or fucking leave it. What Keith showed was that you can have as little technical ability as possible, but if you have buckets of personality, you can play and you will be unique and no one will sound like you, before you or after you. Keith Moon invented his own drumming vocabulary and he used it. I think Keith was from an era that appeals so much to people. He did it all at a time when you could get away with things, and we all want a little bit of that."

Live, The Who were a band on a whole different level.

"Professional ambition–to smash 100 drum kits.

Personal ambition–to stay young forever."

TONY FLETCHER

MUSIC WRITER AND AUTHOR OF DEAR BOY: THE LIFE OF KEITH MOON

"I've been a Who fan since I was about eight or nine years old. I saw The Who perform just the once with Keith, at Charlton football ground in 1976. When I started the book I didn't think I would be the sort of person to write a book about Keith Moon. The story in the back of the book, about meeting him at the ICA in August 1978 at the *Who's Who* fan exhibition, was the start. I had started my fanzine and Keith invited me to take a copy round to his flat in Curzon Place. I went round but he wasn't in and then time ran out and he died before I got the chance to see him again.

"The thing really stuck with me: this really crazy guy, who he was in many ways, had also taken the time out to be really nice to me that day at the ICA. He had reached out and invited some kind of relationship that sadly couldn't develop because he died.

"It was almost two decades later I started *Dear Boy.* By this time I had done a couple of books, and they had been about bands, I had been doing my music fanzine and I had been working as a music journalist. But I felt that I could maybe take on something bigger and I just kept thinking about Keith Moon.

"When I was thinking about doing the book someone told me not to bother because Roger Daltrey was making a movie. As a result I actually left the idea for a couple of years. Then nothing seemed to come of the movie and so I was able to approach Chris Charlesworth [Omnibus Press], who had done my previous book, and he knew Keith Moon personally when he was alive and he knew me well enough so he said he'd like to see me work on the book.

"Things began to come together. I also think there was a clear connection between the time that I had met Keith and how that encounter stuck with me and motivated me to want to tell his story. That was how and why I wrote *Dear Boy.*

"To research *Dear Boy* I spoke to over a hundred people and back then it was really hard work. Over the years people have often asked me how I went about writing the book and I always answer 'you just start', then one contact leads to another, then you approach them and hope the door won't be shut in your face. I met more and more people who saw that I was doing the book for the right reasons and they would open the door for another contact.

"One thing that I think worked to my advantage was that The Who had broken up but at that point of beginning the book they were just reforming. This meant that everyone I approached could sort of act independently. This made things a little easier.

"The timing was also important. I think someone had tried to write a book around 1978/79 but a lot of doors stayed shut. I came along almost 20 years later and a lot of people said, 'You know what, I wouldn't have talked to you 10 or 15 years ago, but now Keith has been dead long enough and I can be honest with you.' There are a lot of people that think it's a good idea to write a book about someone just after they have died; I hope not to be one of those people.

Left: Keith, the charismatic dear boy, at home in Los Angeles, November 1974.

"When I started the book, only a few people had email. I remember I hand-wrote a letter to one of Keith's old school teachers. They replied with a long hand-written letter. Other times I just had to pick people's names out of the phone book and hope that it was the right person I was trying to contact.

"The further I got with the book the closer I felt to Keith Moon. At times it even felt dangerous. I have since spoken to other writers who have experienced a similar thing. When you do a book like *Dear Boy* you do start to get inside Keith Moon's head, which to some degree, you need to, if you're going to take a biography seriously. And Keith Moon was a very complicated character and it wasn't easy trying to figure him out.

"Some days I was working on the book for up to 12 hours a day, easily. And in those 12 hours a day you sort of almost become parts of his personality. I mean only in modest and quite minor ways. But you start thinking, 'Oh I wonder what a brandy champagne cocktail tastes like,' or you might write about how he would sometimes snap at people and I would find myself snapping at someone. So you do find that you can get inside someone's head. I guess it's what actors do for certain parts and taking on personalities. It's the switching off that can sometimes be a little difficult and it can get a little bit dark when you're really engaged in a biography.

"My perception also changed during the course of writing the book. I knew there was more to Keith Moon than the happy go lucky guy, and there was. I discovered some of his unhappiness and he had insecurities. One of the big interviews that I did, and that was near the end of the book, was with his ex-wife, Kim. She invited me to Texas to stay with her and Ian McLagan. So I went and I found out lots of things–some unsavoury–and that was the part that I found hard to like about Keith as a person. I learned about the other side of Keith Moon's personality. But that was only part of Keith's story and it didn't stop me writing the book. Overall I think Keith was a very loveable guy but with insecurities that he sometimes took out on other people."

JOHN PEUTHERER

THE WHOO / WHO 2

"A whole lot of drumming, that's what comes to mind. A whole load of madness, drugs and booze comes to mind too, but it's really about the drumming for me. The drumming was outstanding.

"I was of the Mod revivalist generation, so for me it was all about the bands like The Jam and Secret Affair, who took their inspiration from The Who, and then there was the Two Tone stuff. It was the Two Tone stuff that made me want to play the saxophone, but then I saw *The Kids Are Alright* and within a minute of watching Keith Moon I knew that I wanted to play the drums instead, and that's what I did.

"I suspect that when people stood in front of The Who in the sixties they would have had no idea that people would still be talking about the band and Keith Moon some 50 years later. Keith Moon is one of those guys that sits beside the greats like Jimi Hendrix. They were innovators of their time. I think it's been a real shame that Keith's drumming got overshadowed by the rock'n'roll lifestyle; at least as far as the media documented it. I like to think that had he gotten sober and still been around today, he would be an even more outstanding person and drummer. It's the sheer joy that Keith seemed to play with, I also hear abandonment too. Keith seemed to play so naturally and fluid and I liked that; it was like he didn't have to think too hard about it. Playing drums just flowed out of him and it's so great to watch and listen to. What he did has certainly influenced and inspired me; I mean, listen to Keith's drumming on *Tommy*... and he was only just in his twenties.

"I played at The Who convention in 2013 with my band. I also got involved in organising it too. The Who conventions are a great place where Who fans can gather together from all around the world. The people that attend the convention really 'get' the band and a little bit more. Over the years they have been attended by the likes of Dougal Butler, Chris Charlesworth, Irish Jack and Richard Barnes. Different people tend to organise the events and it seems to work out, and there's always a lot of love for Keith Moon."

DENISE DUFORT

GIRLSCHOOL

"Nutter! Moonie was a brilliant drummer but a nutter. I loved him. My older brother played drums and he was always playing Who records; that's how I came across Keith Moon, then I wanted to be like that and started playing drums when I was about nine.

"When I first started to learn I looked at other drummers like Gene Krupa, Buddy Rich and Cozy Powell and they were showman like Moonie became. I really liked that showmanship and that appealed to me about Moonie.

"I watch footage of Moonie and I just don't know how he does some of the things that he does. I think he must have been mad to play like he did. I think Moonie was very punky, I would say he was one of the first punk drummers. That's how I would describe his style of playing.

"The thing with Moonie was that he put drums in the forefront. Up until him all the other drummers put themselves in the back. I mean most drummers watch drummers onstage but I think Moonie was watched by a lot of people in the audience that weren't drummers. Moonie would mesmerise them; they couldn't help themselves.

"I don't know what happened to him over the years but he did strange things like starting to talk all posh. I think some of the strange stuff overshadows him as a drummer and a musician, but there were many sides to him I suppose. As a drummer he was unique, he had an individual style that no one else has ever had.

"Moonie never used to follow the bass guitar like most drummers do, he followed Townshend's guitar. I think this is what made Moonie's drumming style so unique and brilliant. He would put fills in places that no one would think of putting them. It's great to hear and it made The Who sound the way that they did. No other band has ever sounded like The Who and that was because of Moonie."

Right: Keith, ever the perfect gentleman. Denise Dufort: "He did strange things like starting to talk all posh."

RICHARD COLE

TOUR MANAGER

"I was working as a roadie for Unit Four Plus Two at the time and The Moody Blues had a house party that I went to. There was a guy there called Mike Shaw who was the production manager for The Who and The Merseybeats. Mike offered me a job with The Merseybeats, but I was leaving the following day to go and ponce about in Spain for a few months. But when I came back I called up Mike, asking if the job with The Merseybeats was still going. He told me no, but did say he had one with The Who. I took the job and started working as a roadie for them. This was late 1965.

"I already knew of The Who because I had seen them play at the Scene Club; they were The High Numbers then. The Scene was a Mod club. The Who were good but I only remember them doing early Motown sort of covers. The Scene Club disc jockeys, like Guy Stevens, played a lot of those songs. Some of us didn't think about The Who as a Mod band though. I had started as a Mod in 1961 when I was 15. We would go to the Lyceum and the room was full of little cliques of Mods. After the Lyceum we started going to the Scene. But by late 1964 Mod had basically finished and then The Who came along.

"Around that time of seeing The High Numbers down the Scene I had also met Keith one night in the Flamingo. It was on a night when Ronnie Jones & The Nightimers were playing. I was working for them. That particular night Keith was with Pete [Townshend] and John [Entwistle]; Keith and John would be out together. They were all very different personalities but it worked for their band.

"Being a roadie for The Who meant doing a bit of everything really. I did a lot of driving of the van, with Keith, carrying his drums around. It was often me, Keith and John in the van. They lived quite close to me so that meant I could pick them up. Roger had his own car so would drive himself and Pete would sometimes drive himself or catch the train. My first job meant going to Edinburgh with them. In the early days we all stayed in the same hotels and spent a lot of time together and Keith wasn't much more different to what people wrote about him. I remember that on that trip to Scotland Keith asked me to stop the van because he wanted to go into a hardware store to get something. As he ran inside I asked John what he was after and John just smiled. Keith returned with weed killer and sugar. He used them to make smoke bombs. Even back in those days he was always up to tricks. John was always very quiet but he was like Keith's silent accomplice.

"As a drummer there was nothing else like Keith Moon; he played furiously. He was unusual in so many ways. Just not using the hi-hat is one example. He used all of his drums all of the time. Another unusual thing was that The Who were only a three-piece band. This was unusual because most bands from that era were at least a four piece that included a rhythm guitarist. They moved around on stage a lot; apart from John, he never moved, he was like a statue. Then Townshend would be smashing his guitar into the amps and Daltrey would be swinging his mic around. There were no

Left: "So many tickets down the Scene, honey. They're like to blow a fuse." The Who at the Scene Club, Ham Yard, Soho, 5 August 1964.

barriers in those days and the audience were very close to the band. People had to be careful not to get hit.

"I saw some of the smashing up of the gear but it didn't happen every night. One night in Bishops Stortford I remember he smashed the whole kit up; even the cymbals got broke. We had no replacement drums. Luckily I played drums and had a blue Premier kit (at the time Keith played a red kit). But Keith had to buy my kit from me; I wasn't going to let him smash my kit up. There weren't a lot of drums actually getting smashed up. Mostly Keith would just push them over. But we did have to protect the kit and stop people from stealing parts of it.

"I would try to watch Keith onstage but I had to keep an eye on Townshend too. There were only two roadies; me and Neville Chesters, although I mostly worked on the side of the stage with John, and Neville the side with Townshend. It was different in those days. I mean if Pete broke a guitar string, he had to fix it because Neville didn't know how, and the same with Keith's drums. If a skin needed replacing I didn't know how to do it, Keith had to do it.

"I was with Keith at the Paul McCartney party but by that time I had stopped working for The Who. I had still seen him around in places like LA or New York because I worked for other bands and Keith would come and hang out. I remember visiting Keith in (I think) Bel Air and leaving my Merc convertible on his drive—it rained—and got soaked. I had totally lost all sense of time while being with Keith. This was often the case. Another time Keith and I were hanging out with Jimmy Page. We were in Tramps night club and after we went round to his flat and he played me his drumming on Lionel Bart's *The Hunchback of Notre Dame*. Keith had a tape of it.

"At the McCartney party Keith was with Annette and he looked well. Keith wasn't drinking and there was some talk of getting engaged to Annette. He

Keith and Annette at the Buddy Holly party, 6 September 1978.

was the most subdued that I'd ever seen him. I didn't actually go for the film showing; I left before it started, went home for a bit, then went to Tramps. A guy I knew called Don, who ran Artist Services, came looking for me because Keith had asked him to find 'Richard'. But there was a mix up and Keith was looking for a different Richard; I suspect Richard Dawes, who was working for him at the time.

"The next day I heard on the news that Keith had died and there was some mention of Heminevrin. It came as a shock especially because he had seemed perfectly alright only the night before. In 1984 I was in a treatment centre and was given Heminevrin; in there they were distributed to you, but Keith didn't have that, he'd probably been given a bottle of them. The first time I had even heard of Heminevrin was in 1978 because of its mention in relation to Keith. There wasn't a great deal of information or education around about it. Who knows what really happened. I mean if he was anything like me, when it says take one you automatically think two is going to be better. You find with people that have been taking drugs for a lot of their lives, they don't really take much notice of what it says on the label. Maybe Keith just got confused. I don't know."

RICHARD EVANS

DESIGNER & ART DIRECTOR FOR THE WHO

My first encounter with Keith would have been when as a young art student I booked The Who to play at an art college hop at the Dungeon Club in Nottingham in May 1965.

The group turned up a couple of hours late but we didn't really care as most of us were pissed by then anyway. I can't remember too much about the actual gig but what did stick in my mind were the drummer and the guitarist. They both exuded this fantastic charisma. I'm sure Daltrey and Entwistle did too, but I remember Keith being the most extraordinary drummer in his manner of playing–twirling his sticks, throwing them in the air and catching them with great flair and flourish. He played, or should I say performed like a true showman.

Fast forward another 11 years to 1976 and I was working as the in-house graphics man with Storm [Thorgerson] and Po [Aubrey Powell] at Hipgnosis, the seminal design group, in their tatty studio in Denmark Street in the heart of Soho. I'd been there three or four years and picked up an amazing amount of experience designing covers for the Floyd, Zeppelin, the Pretty Things and Peter Gabriel *et al,* and I felt like I was now ready to set out on my own.

Po and Storm had been asked to come up with the designs for the forthcoming *Who Put The Boot In* shows at Celtic, Swansea and Charlton football grounds. As they were very busy on other projects they had farmed out the poster design to illustrator Bush Hollyhead and they asked me if I would like to design the tour programme as my first freelance

job. I jumped at the chance. I met up with Chris Chappel who worked at Trinifold Management and we set about organising the programme.

Wishing to get away from the traditional style of rock tour book, my concept was to design it like a glossy magazine with some really good content, a sort of *Playboy*-kind of thing and, knowing the reputation The Who had for fun, that it should be very humorous. And so *Bellboy* magazine was born–and of course, Keith just had to be the centre-fold!

Keith was living in Malibu and flew in for rehearsals prior to the shows. He was staying at the Royal Garden Hotel in Kensington and so we arranged to go over and do a photo shoot with him. At the last minute I thought it would be a great idea to also photograph him for the front cover, dressed up in a bellboy's uniform and so I had hired one, complete with pill-box hat and gloves, from Berman & Nathan's, the theatrical costumiers, but I had to take a rough guess at Keith's size.

Back in those days I wasn't confident enough using a Hasselblad camera so I persuaded Storm to come along and take the actual shots. We all turned up at Keith's hotel around lunchtime and knocked on Keith's door. I must admit I was a tad nervous as to what to expect.

The door flew open and Keith welcomed us in with his typical 'dear boy' this and 'dear boy' that – a most congenial host, asking us if we would all like a drink – 'Scotch and Coke, dear boy, Scotch and Coke?' 'You're very kind, Keith but it's just a bit too early in the day for me.'

Annette was there too but pretty much left us to it. The one thing I was immediately aware of was that the room was a complete shambles. There was an up-turned bed-side table on top of the unmade bed and when I went to the bathroom I noticed that the lavatory pan was stuffed with bath towels!

I think we may have done the nude shots of Keith first as I do remember he took a while to 'warm up' for the shoot although he had no inhibitions whatsoever, getting down to his birthday suit in front of us all. He was in pretty good shape with a good California beach boy tan. We did some shots of Keith on the sofa in front of the window, stark naked but realising we should also perhaps photograph him with his 'bits' covered up rather than be arrested by the Old Bill for publishing nude material! We did several frames of Keith holding a black-and-white football and a few of him with Annette's fox fur stole covering his parts. By this time he was getting into the swing of things and was a most obliging 'model'.

We then dressed Keith up in his bellboy outfit but realised that the costume was several sizes too small! He'd put on a bit of weight

with living in California. Fortunately the jacket had velcro fastenings so we managed to squeeze him into it. Handing him a tray of glasses and bottles I instructed him to stand out in the corridor and upon the command enter the room carrying the tray aloft. I said, imagine you've burst into the room and caught a couple *in flagrante*. I must say, he really acted the part brilliantly and we did several takes, each one funnier than the one before.

It's now 40 years since that first job working for The Who and I've always said that that day was my

baptism of fire. Keith was a charming host, a great joiner-inner and a perfect gentleman. In the umpteen times I saw The Who with Keith I never tired of seeing that same showmanship I'd first seen in Nottingam in '65, that amazing lead drumming that he did, his banter and on-stage rapport – particularly with Pete, his enthusiastic but off-key singing and that live -wire exuberance. The fact is, Keith just *loved* being in The Who. I firmly believe that of all the millions of fans The Who have collected over the past 50 years there has never been a bigger Who fan than Keith Moon. Dear boy."

RICHARD NEWMAN
STEVE MARRIOTT & THE OFFICIAL RECEIVERS

the Official Receivers

"Great drummer, that's what comes to mind! I really liked Moonie's flamboyant drumming and the way he played from the heart and meant what he played too. My dad [drummer Tony Newman] was into Moonie so that was how I came across him. My dad hung out with him in the seventies and was always going to parties with him. He was always pointing Moonie out to me. He had a lot of respect for Moonie. I posted some footage of Moonie on Facebook the other day and my dad left the comment 'now that is the real deal.' He has a good story of Moonie, Kenney Jones and himself locking themselves into Air Studios and not letting anyone in until they'd drunk all the beer.

"I don't think The Who would have been The Who without Moonie; he certainly left his mark on the band. I think he led the band too, by the way he played. And when he played you couldn't keep your eyes off of him. The smashing up hotels was a part of who Moonie was but his playing always came first. The thing was, there was no one like him and there never will be again. Keith Moon was a one off.

"It was Steve Marriott who also turned me on to Moonie. I worked with Steve in The Official Receivers for over a year. He was always pointing things out about the way Moonie played. He had a lot of love for Moonie."

GEORGIANA STEELE-WALLER

STUDIO MANAGER AT THE WHO'S RAMPORT STUDIOS

"I first met Keith at the Monterey Pop festival in 1967. I was working as a go-for for Derek Taylor and had been travelling with The Beatles the year before. Because of this connection I met Moonie.

I had been living in LA but in 1969 I moved back to England. One night I went to a club called Revolution in London and Keith came over and said, 'Hey girl, how you doing?' I told him that I was going to Ibiza the following day and he asked why, so I said the sun. He replied 'But I have the sun,' and it turned out he had a big sun on his wall at home. Soon after I got back I started running Ramport Studios in Battersea.

"Seeing The Who in Monterey was the first time that I saw them. I watched from the wings. It was great, they were great days, it was 1967 and everybody seemed to be dropping acid. Watching The Who smash up their instruments, then Hendrix set light to his guitar was quite an experience for me.

"And Keith was totally unique as a drummer. I had known other drummers and had hung out with Ginger Baker, but Moonie just took playing drums to a whole other level. Keith did things on drums that other drummers could only dream about being able to do. He created a whole new sound and he made The Who. Keith Moon made the drummer a star. There had been the jazz greats like Buddy Rich but Moonie made the drummer the star in rock.

"I remember that Zak Starkey used to come to the house (I stayed down at Tara after Kim left) and Keith would show him how to play drums, it was

almost as if he was grooming him to take over his position in The Who someday. Tara could be a perfectly normal house until there was a guest. As soon as there was a guest Keith had to act the loon again. In public he had to make an entrance, he had to be the loon that was expected of him. We would sit down and talk but when it got too serious he would act up. Moonie really was two people. And at the time he was at an age that could keep up with it. It's not something that would have been able to be continued.

"I saw Keith the night before he died. He came to my parents' place, with his new driver. Keith and my parents got on well. They were actors and that was something that Keith was interested in. I had only just flown in and only had a few hours' sleep, but there he was at the door. He came in and I remember that he really wanted to tell my parents how he was getting better and hadn't been drinking. Keith sounded very sincere while he talked about giving up the booze and studying acting, and wanted to be like Ringo and do movies. But then he went to the Buddy Holly thing and that ended his plans.

"I ran into some trouble once and ended up having to go to the Old Bailey. As a result I skipped town and went off to Ibiza and refused to come back. My dad phoned up Moonie asking him if he'd try and get me back. I got, and still have, a telegram from Moonie asking me to return to England and he added 'because London is flagging without you. Love Keith.'

"Keith was a very caring person and in the end I think he was so weary of having to be Moon The Loon. I think he wanted to leave behind all the smashing up hotels and be taken seriously. It was the Keith that I saw in the end. In the end I think he

The Who at the first Monterey International Pop Festival, California, Sunday 18 June 1967.

Keith astride his drum kit at the Gator Bowl in Jacksonville, Florida, on 7 August 1976.

just wanted to settle down, he was ready to settle down with Annette and be normal. I remember him telling me how by the time we would all be 40 we'd all be settled down. It just seemed funny at the time.

"I was down a pub called the Duke of Wellington in Belgravia, London with my dad when I heard about Keith dying. The phone rang, which wasn't unusual; my mother would often call asking when we would be back for dinner. That day my dad answered and when he came back he ordered me a large brandy. He told me that it had been Kitty on the phone and she wanted to let us know that Keith had died. I went home and played 'Bell Boy'. Keith's death came not long after a drinking session in a venue down the Fulham Road. I had been sat next to Ginger Baker and even while Ginger was himself living out on the edge he said to me, 'Georgiana, you need to rein Keith in because he is going to kill himself.' Ginger and a lot of people (already living on the edge) sensed something. I will remember Moonie for many reasons and I hope he will be remembered for being a better drummer rather than a lunatic."

JOHNNY ECHOLS

LOVE

"Keith Moon was a fantastic drummer, I didn't know him personally, but I certainly knew about his drumming. Myself and the other members of Love were very familiar with The Who and what they were doing. Don Conka had some similar attributes to Keith but Keith was something else, and he had more notoriety. It really doesn't surprise me that people are still very interested in Keith Moon because he did some excellent work; it's the same for others such as John Coltrane and Elvin Jones, those guys were exceptional and they did stuff that was timeless."

Love, 1969. L–R: Johnny Echols, Arthur Lee (top) Bryan MacLean (centre), Kenny Forssi and Michael Stuart-Ware.

Keith perched on a somewhat battered Ferrari Dino at Tara, his home in Chertsey, Surrey, with daughter, Mandy (left), and some of the cars (and hovercraft) in his collection, 17 October 1972. Not seen in this photograph is his fully furnished milk float (see page 55).

KIERON MAUGHAN

AUTHOR OF ROCK STARS' CARS

"Keith was an unfortunate driver who only drove occasionally. Instead he had three drivers; the most famous being 'Dougal' Butler, who has the most detailed stories. There are many myths that surround Keith and his cars. The myth regarding the car in the swimming pool isn't correct. It was alleged that on his 21st birthday a Lincoln Continental was driven in to the pool. However, people that were actually at the party say that pretty much everything else was thrown in the pool, including people, sun loungers, tables and waitresses, but not a Lincoln Continental.

"It seems that as the legend of the car in the pool grew Keith also started to quote it, which just added to the legend. But it never actually happened. It couldn't have anyway. The myth has been busted as it's been proven that when you try to open a car door under water, you have to have a window open, otherwise the pressure is too much and the door won't open. All the same it's a good story and it added something to the Oasis album cover for *Be Here Now*. Keith did however drive one of his Rolls-Royces into the pond at Tara by accident. And more than likely he would just leave the cars there with the keys still in the ignition and go and do something else.

"There are some amazing accounts in Dougal's book *Full Moon* about Keith's cars being driven through fences and over-ending his AC 428 by changing from drive to first at about 100 miles an hour (you just don't do that with an automatic).

"John Mears was another of Keith's drivers. It was John who was tasked with going to get Keith's Roller painted lilac. Roger Daltrey's account is that Keith had the Roller hand-painted, but he didn't. Instead John Mears was given a few hundred quid to get the car painted locally in London.

"Before that particular Rolls-Royce, Keith owned a Bentley. It had a record player in it. It was one of the first cars to have a record player in it. It was similar to a CD player in modern cars. You had to slip a seven-inch record into a hole and it would play. I suspect Keith had seen George Harrison's and Mick Jagger's and decided that he wanted one too.

"I think by 1968/69 Keith got the bug for having nice cars and at some points he owned several cars at the same time. Keith was also one of the first big rock musicians to openly court the press to gain publicity and have good relationships with them. The Beatles and the Stones had been pushed around by the Epstein and Loog Oldham machines and had kept a distance but Keith was inviting journalists around to his house. There just wasn't anything as personal as that. And that was Keith. There were always journos and police hanging around Tara. That was partly how Keith was able to get away with so much for so long. The local bobby would just tip him off when he was being too noisy.

"Keith lived his life at such a pace, just like his cars, just like everything that he did. He even gave one of his cars to three bikers to have a go and they drove it around the corner and smashed it up.

"Keith did own Bentleys and Rollers but in some of the photos you can see of Keith sitting in flash cars, they weren't actually his cars; he would sometimes borrow them to make himself look richer. Often the media paid for the hire of the cars; it made for a better photo shoot.

"What happened to some of Keith's cars is a question that hasn't been answered. The lilac Rolls-

Royce has never been found. I've been searching for it for years. The likelihood is that it was broken for spares. The AC 428 is still around. His white Corniche Roller I've been searching for too. There is a guy who says he has a Ferrari that Keith owned but nobody believes Keith owned a Ferrari. It may be that he owned it briefly but had to return it for financial reasons or it was a Keith Moon that owned it but it wasn't the Keith Moon of The Who; it was just someone with the same name.

"I saw a Ferrari log book once that had a Keith Moon signature (and he used several) but the address is not Curzon Place but a place literally just around the corner. It's unlikely that Keith had that car at that time because it was dated just when he returned from America and he had no money. He hadn't sold the Malibu home by this point. But maybe the record company bought it for him. It's possible, because he had demanded money in the past to buy expensive things. That log book was transferred to another person a few months after Keith apparently owned the car. There are lots of mysteries where Keith and cars are concerned. Regarding Keith's American cars, well, they are probably still out there. They are hard to track down. But the Excalibur is possibly still around, but the Lincoln Continental not so.

"In my own research for my *Rocks Stars' Cars* project I found that drummers were the most forthcoming. People like Keith Moon and John Bonham were all-powerful drummers and they wanted all-powerful cars. I don't think Keith was especially a petrol head but in his time he did go and buy some absolute gems."

Right: Keith dressed as Scrooge for Disc and Music Echo *Christmas edition, London, 14 December 1970. He is standing outside The Old Curiosity Shop in Westminster, which is believed to have been the inspiration for the antique shop in the Dickens novel of that name.*

BRAD ROGERS

WHO COLLECTOR

"I was a fan of The Who, then about 20-something years ago a friend of mine gave me some old albums. There were some rare pieces among them and I liked that. From there I moved on to collecting posters from venues that The Who played at. Then it progressed from there and I started checking out the auctions and discovered that I could buy a Keith Moon drum. As the years passed I built up quite a collection. Collecting really is a fun hobby, everybody should have a hobby, some people like to fish some people like to play golf, my hobby was collecting Who memorabilia. If you're a collector it doesn't matter what it is; it's all about the thrill of the hunt.

"The first Keith Moon item that I bought was one of the bass drum skins from the Pictures of Lily kit. I got this from one of the roadies that had been with the band. A year or so after that a floor tom

One of the drum skins used by Keith during The Who's show at the Saville Theatre, London, on 22 October 1967.

from that same kit came along at one of the Sotheby sales. I got that in 1993. I managed to collect most of the pieces from that kit that came on the market during that time. In all I got three floor toms, a top tom and the bass drum skin. The conventional wisdom is that the bass drums were either discarded or lost or maybe even The Who has them in storage somewhere. The Victoria & Albert museum in London have some tom-toms on display and I know another collector has a tom.

"Over the years I have loaned some of my Keith Moon pieces to places like the Rock'n'roll Hall of Fame in Cleveland, Ohio. It's nice to have other people enjoy and get some satisfaction out of them. Now I have three toms on display at the Musical Instrument Museum in Phoenix, Arizona.

"I mostly focused on getting parts from the

Above: A 14 x 8 tom-tom. Right: a 16 x 18 floor tom previously owned by Keith's mum Kitty and his sister Lesley.

Pictures of Lily kit because I found it to be the most appealing and the most charming. I had a couple of cymbals at one point but have since sold them off. I have some of Keith's drum sticks and a set of claves too that Keith used on 'Magic Bus'. I had one of his Esso jumpsuits but I sold that to Christie's a few years back. I also have Keith's gold disc for *Who's Next*; at one time I had three, the other two were *Tommy* and *Quadrophenia*. Over the years I have been asked where I have got some of the stuff from. There's lots of places, from auctions to other collectors. One of the pieces in my collection I bought direct from Mandy [Keith's daughter] and another piece I bought directly from Keith's mum [Kitty]. It's my opinion that those two saw that the drums could remain together. I think they saw me as a collector who would try and put as much of the kit together as possible. In other words they would go to a good home and not be exploited.

"I first became a Keith Moon fan when I got into The Who around the time of the *Who's Next* album. I was one of the *Who's Next* generation. *Who's Next* and *Quadrophenia* were the albums that I got introduced to. The first time I saw them live was in 1976, in Denver, Colorado. By this time The Who were a very popular band in the States. In the mid-seventies they were on top of the world. In my view this was the band's most productive time.

"If I had to choose a word to describe Keith Moon as a drummer and a musician I would choose 'unique'. He had a great unique drumming style that worked for The Who. He was much more than just an anchor for the band; he almost led the band too. I think Keith stretched the boundaries of what his role as a drummer was. I think he was also one of the first drummers to expand the kit away from the typical format. And when Keith did it, he did it in a big way. As time passed his kits got bigger and bigger, which today people can take for granted but back then it was a very novel concept. It was cutting edge at the time."

Another Go Exclusive

Direct from Britain, exclusive to GO, is this picture series of the wildest drum kit around. Above, Keith Moon of the Who selects the final artwork with the help of Jeffrey Hurst, creative director of Premier Drums' advertising agency.

Keith Moon...

The kit is almost finished, but Keith is there to make sure everything is exactly the way he wants it. Listening to Keith's comments is Phil Franklin, Premier's promotion manager.

Britain's Patent

The psychedelic outfit is finished, and Keith sits proudly in the driver's seat. The $5000 kit is creating a lot of comment during the Who's current tour of the States.

Exploding Drummer

MATTHEW BRAIM

THE CLIQUE

"It was 1981, I was a first year weedy grammar school nerd. I'd just been taken to see *Dance Craze*, the film about the Two Tone and ska movement, which arose in the late seventies /early eighties on the back of the huge, ubiquitous Mod revival. I had decided I was a Mod ever since The Who's film *Quadrophenia* came out in 1979, kick-starting the whole revival, despite only having my parents' sixties records to listen to, and one Ben Sherman button-down (they did kids' sizes) to my name. However, my pocket-money purchase of the Jam's single 'Going Underground' confirmed my Mod status, at least to me.

Then I did two things almost simultaneously. I bought the book *Moon The Loon*, by Peter 'Dougal' Butler, about the life of Keith Moon, whose shiny red cover in a newsagent's book carousel caught my child's eye, and with my birthday money I bought The Who's *My Generation* album, which Virgin records had recently rereleased.

"I read about the insane, ultimate rock star – part genius, part madman, part hilarious wit (as a weedy nerd, I admired wit to avoid death by bullying). What I heard was astonishing! The sound of Keith Moon's drumming throughout the *My Generation* album, and how it combined with the other instruments, on first hearing was possibly THE most exciting thing I have ever heard. It was powerful, loud, aggressive – everything I wasn't – but also (to my ears) highly complex and difficult. Not only that, but according to the book, which I read cover to cover six times non-stop, the man who created these sounds seemed to be (and indeed was) the epitome of the bad boy rock star! From that moment I wanted to play the drums.

"By sheer luck my younger brother had just taken up drum lessons at school and soon he got an old Premier kit (like Keith Moon played!). We were also lucky enough to have an actual 'music room' in our house – a room filled with various instruments, stereo equipment and very basic recording decks.

"Every chance I got, it was on with the huge black headphones, crank up the stereo and play along to every bit of vinyl by The Who I could find. I learned not only how to play drums, but how to play in a band. From the genius of John Entwistle's bass playing I learned how music worked, from Pete Townshend and Roger Daltrey I discovered the excitement of powerful, discordant rock music, and from Keith Moon I gained an insight into the sheer joy of being alive. Because I have never, in the 33 years since, felt so totally alive as when I am somewhere in the world behind my (Premier, of course) kit, playing music I love, in a band in front of crowds of happy people. And I owe my blessed life entirely to the unique brilliance of Mr Keith Moon."

Ringo and Keith in Los Angeles, April 1974.

BINKY PHILIPS

THE PLANETS

"**Keith was The Who. In a very real tangible musical way, everything about The Who allowed Keith's savant-genius to flourish unimpeded, only aided and abetted.**

"Noel Gallagher of Oasis really boiled Keith down to five words: the Jimi Hendrix of drummers. I am madly in love with Ringo, the most underrated musician of all time. Charlie Watts is a pure hero to me. Bonham was The Rascals' Master Dino Danelli's greatest disciple. But Keith Moon? The mould was broken BEFORE they made him. An ADHD savant-virtuoso. His style has been described as the sound of a drum set down a staircase. Add to that a technique of inhuman ability. One listen to 'Young Man Blues' on *Live At Leeds* is enough.

"I would occasionally read *Downbeat* magazine back then. A pure jazz publication, I would read the interviews with jazz giants I barely knew anything about just because they were so opinionated and sick-knowledgeable. Both Elvin Jones and Tony Williams, two of jazz's monolithically monumental drummers by anyone's standards, in separate interviews, both cited 'that guy in The Who' as the only rock drummer that impressed them. To be fair, Elvin also mentioned Ringo.

"One of The Who's most significant sonic qualities came for the fact that all three instrumentalists had deliberately exaggerated their high end. While Townshend and Entwistle's guitars rumbled and thundered, both had a very raw, almost brittle top end to their sound. Add to that the fact that Keith, ever the complete rule breaker, rode on crash cymbals. This alone created a white noise wash across the sonic spectrum of The Who, akin to a jet engine, as Roger described Moon's playing the first time he sat in with him, Pete and John on Bo Diddley's 'Road Runner', also the song where Pete 'discovered' his patented string-scrape with his pick.

"While a drummer will likely wince at this absurd reductivism, there are really only two kinds of cymbals: thick and thin. The thicker, the deader, the more useful to 'ride' on, a more open looser feel than keeping your 4/4 tempo on the open/close hi-hat cymbals. The thinner the cymbal, the louder, the splashier, which means the shorter the duration. Keith didn't bother with ride cymbals. He had three cymbals out front and one over his floor toms. All four were crashes.

"Combine the three layers of aural assault levels of sizzling high end and, while you heard the music clearly, there was this sonic element that was just, well, intimidating, uniquely aggressive. An aural assault!

"Truly, The Who's music/act was almost a weapon. They took the stage with something akin to an invasion/occupation. It was theirs now until they didn't want it anymore. Okay!? That Abbie Hoffman chose this band to interrupt at Woodstock indicates that poor Abbie was indeed tripping on that fuckin' brown acid.

"Over the decades, Pete has had many a wonderful, provocative quote. But, if I had to choose only one, it would be from a Nik Cohn article in *Eye* magazine, early 1968... 'We never let the music get in the way of the show.' Chiselled in granite! And it was Keith who led the way!

"The Who were on America's *Shindig*, very early, doing their debut single 'I Can't Explain'. It's a very famous clip now. You can see for yourself, the show's director had his camera guys trained on Moon the whole song. The drummer! I VIVIDLY recall being astonished by Keith more than any other aspect of the band. No one had seen anyone like Keith before. Only Mr Dynamite himself, James Brown, was more animated. And the band was performing live and you could hear through your crappy TV speaker that this wild drummer was hitting the drums really hard and playing super fancy stuff pretty much through the whole song. He also had a strange way of hitting his cymbals, kind of deliberately childish while playing what was obviously ultra-skilful drumming. At 12 years old, I recall, for the first time ever, being even a little intimidated by a band. The three up front looked either angry or bored while this sort of crazed, rubber-faced elf beat the crap out of his drums and the song.

"The Who were the first band to sonically declare the end of The Tyranny of The Singer. The Who made the decision that all four instruments, voice, guitar, bass, drums, were the lead instrument. With Keith in the band, it wasn't even really a choice. Once he sat behind the kit, the other three were in the fight of their lives to be heard and even noticed. His playing and persona are one. As he himself put it, he was The Best Keith Moon-Style Drummer of all time. He now resides in rock's DNA.

"Does it surprise me that there is still so much interest in Keith Moon? No! Keith was made up by a garish screenplay writer... except he wasn't. 'Force of nature' and 'Larger than life' are the merest descriptive phrases for Keith, not vaguely hyperbole. If you look at the, frankly, very, very few acts whose music and reputation continue to grow and thrive decades after their halcyon days, The Who reside comfortably among The Beatles, Rolling Stones, Jimi Hendrix, Led Zeppelin... as befits a band that, for a brief while, were the single most exciting and innovative musical act on planet Earth."

Above: Carnage! Right: Keith, as Uncle Ernie, astride the enormous custom-built Wurlitzer organ on the Tommy *film set, 1974.*

MATTHEW J BRADLEY

DRUMMER IN 'DAD-ROCK' BAND RESON8

"**Christmas 1973, I was given a plastic record player as a present.** I already had some kiddy records and as a three-year-old I really enjoyed music. Over the coming months and years various relatives gave me records. These were mainly 45 rpm singles from the sixties that they didn't want any more. I became a big fan of sixties pop music and would get more of these old records from jumble sales and similar. By the late seventies/early eighties I had moved onto an ageing Dansette-style record player and expanded my love of music into the material that was popular at the time, but still liking the sixties. This fondness for such music came from having all these old records but also partly from the influence of my parents being twenty-somethings in the sixties and that an uncle was in a band that had moderate success in the sixties. However certain bands stuck out from this collection of music, none more so than The Who. My love of music generally made me try out various instruments and by my 14th birthday I found I had a natural flare for things of a percussive nature. In the autumn of 1984 this young lad from the British Midlands took up the drum sticks and has never looked back. I have these early influences, especially the flamboyant style of Keith Moon, to thank for giving me the drive to be the drummer I am today.

"After 30 years of playing I have covered many styles and genres but I'm definitely a rock and pop man. My jazz playing isn't too bad either. As I learned to play the drums I took lessons from the drummer from my uncle's band, but when polishing my skills at home I would place that Dansette by my floor tom and stack up those sixties singles and attempt to play along to the drummers of the sixties, including the legend himself, Keith Moon, and his style was a particular challenge. Having only been playing for about a year I wanted to play in the same style as Keith. Other challenges I set myself were to be a drummer somewhere near Mitch Mitchell, Ginger Baker or jazz legend Buddy Rich. I'm not sure if I'm there or not but my wife has heard music by The Who and the bands these others were in and has queried if it was one of my demos. If you find my material on the internet you can hear the effect of having these influences on the way I play. I copy the light and shade that Keith Moon did and try to copy his energy. I have put into all the types of music I play the exuberance of Keith's playing and have proven that the drummer bloke at the back is just as much a vital part of the band as anyone else. I have heard bands live that I used to be in and the music seems empty and lifeless, just as much as I'd imagine those early Who classics would sound without Keith. I have even seen Who tribute bands and thought that their drummer is not doing Keith any justice, even to the point my elder brother said that I should get up there and show them how it is done!

"Currently I'm a drummer in a 'Dad-Rock' band and part of our catalogue of songs includes some Who material. I am proud to say that you can't tell the difference in the drum part from me in 'Substitute' to that of the original record performance from Keith. In other bands I have used

Left: The view from behind Keith's kit, looking out.

Keith's influence and style to shape the general sound of the band, such as the bands I was in during the nineties and the early 2000's. Listening to songs by Moneypenny, which went on to become Light Vessel Automatic and the girl-fronted Molochai, you will most definitely hear the style and flavour of Keith Moon. I find that the style of Keith's drum playing shows how a regular pattern of rhythm can be punctuated and filled out more than just ticking along with a standard 4/4 time signature.

"When I create a drum part for original material or learn a cover number, once the basics have been mastered I then use my 'Keith Moon mode' to work out how to make the drum part more interesting and give it my own mark. Although my Dad-Rock band Reson8 does classic rock covers I use my Keith influenced style of drum playing to fill out the general sound, as we're a three piece with vocals. I also believe that trying to emulate the style of Keith Moon has made approaching other music material an easier task, as I'm naturally used to playing in an energetic way and I don't find myself struggling to copy drum parts in songs I have to learn.

"As a school teacher for a day job I get asked by students who are learning drums or learning songs how to play certain parts or all of it. Many have been left agog when I step in to show how it is done and play the song with the rest of the student band, almost drum note perfect, especially when I had a go at 'My Generation' and 'I Can See For Miles'. In my music career I have been asked questions on how I play things, including what double bass drum pedal I use. Answers are simple: I don't use a double bass drum pedal, just a single one, and go and listen to how Keith Moon does his drumming on records by himself and The Who. This includes when giving drum lessons, Keith is always given as someone to listen to, to develop skill, style and endurance in drum playing. Thanks Keith, I owe you much."

Left: Keith in gold lamé, onstage with Sha Na Na at the Crystal Palace Bowl, London, June 1972.

The Who onstage in the rain at Swansea Football Club, Vetch Field, Swansea, 12 June 1976.

SCOTT 'PINETOP' PETERSON

QUIVERING RHYTHM HOUNDS

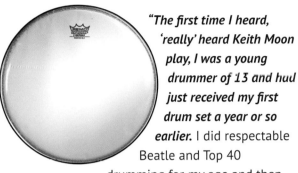

"The first time I heard, 'really' heard Keith Moon play, I was a young drummer of 13 and had just received my first drum set a year or so earlier. I did respectable Beatle and Top 40 drumming for my age and then things changed dramatically. I heard 'I Can See For Miles' for the first time blasting out of my dad's Ford's little four-inch speaker, although it sounded like it was at least 12 speakers. The drums were like nothing I'd ever heard; all over the map but perfect for this song. It sounded like three guys playing one set. My first three thoughts were: Who is this guy? What is he doing? And how is he doing that? It sounded as if he had four arms and a brain of controlled chaos. Little did I know I'd be playing that song in a show band in the mid-seventies.

"I'd heard the first few songs The Who released in the States but nothing affected me like that. I knew immediately that someday I wanted to play like this. Or try. In 1967, 'must see' music in the USA on the telly was *The Smothers Brothers Comedy Hour*. We saw that The Who were to appear on the programme on 10 September 1967, shortly after the Monterey Pop Festival. Finally, I could see this drummer play! My theory at the time was, if I could see what they were doing, I could likely play it, or get close. If that failed, I'd put my finger on the record, slowing it down to better hear the drums.

"That theory went out the window when I saw the show and this massive (for the time) hand painted drum set with what appeared to be a windmill run amok on high gear playing them. Even though they lip synched it, this was no normal drummer and I was forever changed. The next song was 'My Generation', played live, ending with destruction of equipment on American telly for the first time, leaving shrapnel-wounded Moon and a nearly-deafened Pete Townshend onstage with two dumbfounded TV hosts. I was mortified and mesmerised. I had to try and learn this. Obviously there were none of the technical aids we have now, I couldn't watch the programme again, and there was nothing to record the performance with so I just 'went for it'. It sounded like bowling balls rolling down the stairs. When I did the 'finger on the record trick', it slowed down to mere mortal drumming, not the 'slow motion' drum sound I desired.

"Moon's style had no rock'n'roll backbeat, no surf beat (even though he was mad about such music), no 'fatback' drums as we had in soul music at the time, or any semblance of a blues shuffle – none of the genres we American kids had grown up listening to. It was as if he was essentially simultaneously hitting every drum he had while maintaining some sense of timing, meter and tempo. In short, it was the work of a genius; likely a mad genius, but pure genius.

"By 1968, I had a double bass set and by 1973, when I started playing professionally, I bought a set of Royal Purple Premier Drums, all because of Moon. Even in the nightclub bands I played in, I always threw in flourishes of Moon to the best of my ability. His tom rolls, fills and cymbal swells are still epic.

"I'd also started reading everything I could about him in drummer magazines, trade publications, teen magazines... anything. I was as captivated by his persona as I was his talent. I knew Cherry Bombs [drums] very well, and set about

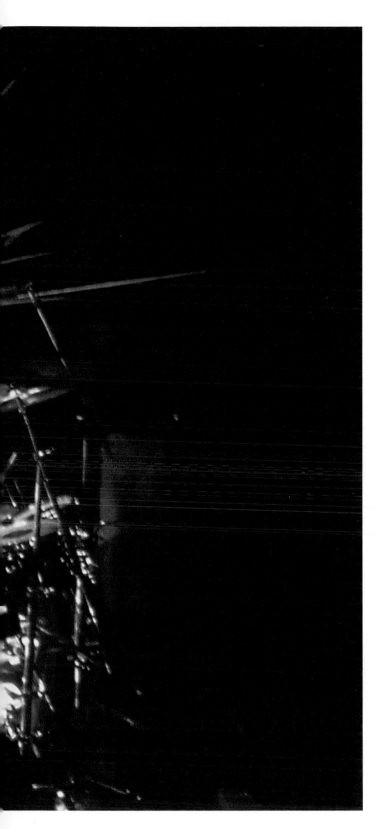

mimicking him for quite a while. Except on the drums. I tried, but nobody plays like Moon did.

"By the mid-seventies we were doing well and added a sixties 'show' to our normal repertoire – essentially an hour medley of songs from 1967 or so, ending with 'I Can See For Miles', complete with smoke machines, flaming drum sticks and ending with me standing on the kit and leaping over it for the last note finale. It seemed like something Moon would do.

"I can honestly say, in 40-plus years of playing, it's the hardest song I ever tried to learn. Actually, not so much 'learn'; it's the hardest song I ever played and tried to make sound remotely authentic. I never learned to read music but it wouldn't have mattered in a song like that, for it would've looked like a squadron of flies splattered onto a page of blank sheet music at supersonic speed. Music like that comes from the soul and a realm in our minds few of us possess.

"After reading Moonie's original biography, someone recently asked me why I thought no movie on Moon had been made as it seemed all that 'late' rock legends had one out. I thought about it and replied, 'No actor can play drums anywhere near Moon's level and no drummer could act well enough to capture the dear boy's image. The special effects have not yet been invented to combine the two. Likely never will be.'

"Perhaps that's why he's still so popular and relevant today; because he's frozen in time in our memories at Monterey, Woodstock, Isle of Wight or from the telly and because nobody alive has the talent and personality combined to unseat him let alone replace him."

Left: Keith with John Wolff during filming of The Kids Are Alright, *Shepperton Studios, May 1978.*

LAWRENCE STREMBA

DRUMMER AND LIFE-LONG WHO FAN

"I was about 17 years old when I heard my first Who song and after that I was hooked. I never heard a drummer drum like Keith before. I had to have all The Who albums and I got them after years of searching – I didn't have internet at the time so I had to do it the hard way. After I got all the albums I needed to learn how to play the drums. When I was 20 I got my first set and I used to try and try and try to drum like Keith; no one can as he was one of a kind, but when I play I just pretend I'm Keith and I do his rolls and I just love it. The Who and Keith Moon inspired me to play and I wasn't even born when they were at their best, so what does that tell you about Keith's greatness? He was the best and always will be in my opinion."

Above and right: Ever the showman, even when leaving the stage.

KAITLIN HAWK

KEITH MOON LOOK-ALIKE

"Some people say that everyone has a twin out there. I believe it! I have one, and it's Keith Moon. My name is Kaitlin Hawk, and I'm a 20-year-old from Florida. The first time I ever saw a photo of Keith, I was shocked by his physical resemblance to me! I was instantly intrigued, and had to know more about this man. The deeper I dug into his life, the more uncanny everything seemed to become. Not only do we look nearly identical, we also have many intimate things in common, such as our personalities, personal situations throughout our lives, mind-sets, and similar childhoods. Keith passed away 17 years before I was born, and then 17 years later, I ultimately discovered who Keith was and how fantastic and iconic a musician he was!

I've always been fascinated by drums, but art is my main passion. We are both very creative people, and I find it insane how much we have in common. People confront me all of the time to tell me how much they think I resemble him, and it never fails to make me smile. I love Keith dearly and hold him very close to my heart. He truly is the twin brother I never had."

Who's who? Kaitlin Hawk, above, and Keith, right.

Keith Moon, one of the most creative and unique players in our profession.

EDDIE TUDURI

SIDEMAN WITH, AMONG OTHERS, DELANEY BRAMLETT, BOBBY WHITLOCK, THE BEACH BOYS, DOBIE GRAY, DEL SHANNON, RICK NELSON & THE STONE CANYON BAND, KENNY LOGGINS, DR JOHN, IKE TURNER, RONNIE HAWKINS AND FOUNDER OF THE RHYTHMIC ARTS PROJECT

"The first thing that comes to mind is Keith's uniqueness as a player. There has never been anyone else like him, before or after. Keith was a big fan of the Stone Canyon bands like Rick Nelson—you wouldn't think it but he was, and that was how I met him because I was drumming for Rick in the early seventies. Keith would come and see us play and we would hang out. Keith used to pick me up (he had someone driving for him back then too) and we would drive out to East LA and just hang out.

"At the time I was being endorsed by a drum company called Camco. Camco was an American company based in Oakland, Illinois. I called them and told them that they should make some drums for Keith, so they did. The kit had to be made using specific measurements and materials so that he could stand on it and throw it about.

"Now here's a thing, I'm kind of a rudimental drummer; I have some prowess in that area. One day we found some drums and I played a bit and then said to Keith, 'Hey Keith, try this.' But he declined saying, 'I'm not going to play after you've played.' I was really taken aback because this was Keith Moon, one of the most creative and unique players in our profession, telling me that he couldn't follow me. I also don't think Keith knew how good a drummer he actually was. I just don't believe he gave himself enough credit as a drummer. Whenever I would try to compliment him

he would just kinda look down.

"When I think about Keith Moon I don't think about the crazy and wild stories, I think about how humble he was. Keith was a really humble and respectful guy. During the times that I hung out with Keith I found him to be a very down-to-earth guy. People write about the crazy stuff but to me it's just a load of MTV garble but there's many of us that don't care to know how many televisions Keith threw out of a hotel window and how many toilets exploded. That stuff is not important.

"Another interesting thing is that I don't think Ricky Nelson was ever given the credit that he was due. He did get it from some of his peers like Kris Kristoffersen and Freddy Fender—these guys really embraced him—but I don't think a lot of people did. And yet Keith Moon would show up at our shows and tell us that he was a big fan. I think Keith had a great deal of substance to his approach to music. I appreciated that in him.

"I first knew about The Who because of the British invasion in the mid-sixties. At the time I was living in New York City and my band used to rehearse in a room above where *The Ed Sullivan Show* was filmed. At that time all the British bands were brought over to appear on *The Ed Sullivan Show* – The Beatles, The Moody Blues, Peter & Gordon and so on. The Who was another that I saw arrive.

The Rhythmic Arts Project started up after I broke my neck in a body surfing accident. As a result of the accident my drumming career had to be put on the shelf for a period of time. I was paralysed, and coming back from that I had to relearn everything. It took some time but I'm now playing again. It was during my own recovery that I developed the programme that would help people who had also suffered similar injuries. The programme developed and now we also work with people with intellectual differences like autism, Down's syndrome and developmental disabilities. We use many things to help these people and drums are integral to this. The programme is supported by friends from the musical world and I bet Keith would have been one of our supporters. That was the kind of guy he was; this was the Keith Moon that I knew.

Check out our website: www.traponline.org."

A 1974 press ad for Keith's single of Brian Wilson's 'Don't Worry Baby'.

RAY DREDGE

SCHOOLFRIEND AND NEIGHBOUR

"I grew up in Wembley, around the area of Chaffey Road, where Keith also grew up – he lived down Chaplin Road. In the fifties the area wasn't especially multicultural, like it was in other parts of London. The boxer Henry Cooper had a greengrocer's shop in Wembley High Road and there was the old Wembley Stadium, so that meant the area was often busy at the weekends.

"I went to the Park Lane Primary School, which was a three-mile walk, but when I was 11 I went to Alperton Secondary Modern School for Boys, which was in Ealing Road. Keith also went there; we were in the same class. The girls went to the Alperton Secondary Modern School for Girls and that was on the other side of a hill. We called that hill the one tree hill and the pupils from both schools would go and meet on it at lunch time.

"Even at school Keith had a reputation as being the funny guy. He would do anything that would draw attention to himself. He didn't do things in a harmful way, but he did lots of silly things, just to get noticed. He really was the joker of the class and because of this he was fun to be around.

"We were at the secondary school in the mid- to late-fifties. It was a great time because when we weren't mucking about down by the canal or playing football in the parks we were discovering the new music that was coming in. Rock'n'roll and Teddy Boys were very popular. We went to the local youth clubs that were held in schools but when we got older we went to the 2I's in Old Compton Street and then the Starlight Ballroom, a large venue on the edge of Wembley. Most of the time our mothers played bingo there, but on one occasion The Birds [Ronnie Wood's group] played there. By the early sixties we were getting into the British R&B bands like The Yardbirds and The Rolling Stones. It was a time when every youngster felt they wanted to be in a band. Out of us, Keith, did and of course went on to play with The Who.

"I didn't see Keith after we left Alperton; lots of us just drifted in different directions because we went to work. In 1960 I got into the Mod thing and got a scooter and on a few occasions I got on the *Ready Steady Go!* TV show, which was filmed in the Wembley area. I remember seeing The Who on *RSG!*"

Keith aping away, centre front, in a Barham Primary School photo.

CRAIG GILL

INSPIRAL CARPETS

inspiral carpets

"Keith Moon was one of the first people that I looked to when I started to play the drums. When I was about 12 my dad took me to see one of the big bands and their drummer was Eric Delaney, who was completely mind-blowing. I had just discovered The Who and Keith Moon too and listening to these guys was totally off-putting because you just couldn't imitate them. As a result, I looked for inspiration from other drummers that were more basic or rudimental. I listened to Mike Joyce of The Smiths because his style was a lot easier to copy. But Keith Moon has got to be in any drummer's top three. He was a great showman but there was so much more. There's myth that his technical ability wasn't that much and he could be sloppy in places. But in Townshend's book he talks about how Moon had to play along to click-tracks and he would do it perfectly, which as drummers know is not an easy task. Drummers tend to simplify what they do when they play along to clicks but if you listen to Moon he doesn't. Listen to the drumming on 'Baba O'Riley', its spot on. When he played he made drumming look effortless too.

"I loved Moon's style but I just found his drumming overwhelming. And this was in the days before things like YouTube where now you can slow things down and see what he was doing. But before this was possible I would look at Moon and think his drumming just came from another planet.

"When I joined Inspiral Carpets I thought, well I'm not going to be the best drummer in the world but I can be the best drummer for the Inspirals. And I got better as time went by and returned to listening to the greats. I recently read Pete Townshend's book and he said that Moon's main influences were Buddy Rich and Eric Delaney and it was Delaney who influenced Moon to try using the double bass drums.

"I actually possess Keith Moon's will. I was looking through *Record Collector* a few years back and someone was selling one of his wills so I bought it. I bought it thinking it was something I could just frame but when it arrived it was about 30 pages long and full of legal spiel. Interestingly, he wasn't able to leave much – his legacy really is in his music and his drumming, there was very little left to his estate. Keith Moon was ideal for The Who. I think certain drummers are meant to be with certain bands and Moon and The Who are an obvious example."

Left: What the roadie saw. Backstage in 1974.

PAUL KEMP

WHO'S WHO

"The greatest rock'n'roll drummer who ever walked on this planet, that's what comes to mind when I think about Keith Moon. I have been playing drums for 36 years and it all started because of Keith Moon. At the time I was into the Mod movement that was happening at the time (1978/79) and that came about as Keith had also died and *Quadrophenia* hit the cinemas.

"When I was learning to play the drums I looked to other drummers but I found Keith to be the most exciting. He was such a spontaneous drummer too, and that I liked. Before Who's Who I played in a string of bands, then someone suggested I form a Who tribute band because of the way that I played drums. So around 1994 I put a few adverts around and the band eventually formed.

"Who's Who built up a good reputation and even John Entwistle came to see us play before he died. This was at the 1998 Who convention. There were others there too, like John Schollar, who Keith played with in The Beachcombers, one of Keith's sisters, and Chris Charlesworth and 'Dougal' Butler. In fact Chris and 'Dougal' were crying into their pints when they watched me play the drums the way that I did. I saw Chris recently at another Who convention and he told me that I was the closest thing to Keith Moon.

"Often drummers ask me if they can have lessons, so they can learn to play in the style that I do. I have to tell them that to do so they would have to unlearn everything that they know about playing the drums. From the start I watched and listened to Keith, so I didn't really learn the standard ways. And Keith just didn't play like a normal drummer. For example, when Keith went into a roll he would work outwards from the kit, starting with the snare, rather than with a tom. Keith also played his two bass drums in a non-standard way. He would play the right hand bass drum like any other drummer and play the left bass drum to fill in the gaps. But Keith would often put his beater through the right bass drum skin because he was so heavy footed. What he would then do is place his right foot on the left hand bass drum pedal and continue while one of his roadies would slip a new drum skin onto the right hand bass drum. But when both bass drums were working Keith would often use the left hand bass drum to lead the bar, and this is unusual because most drummers use the right.

"Keith Moon would also concert tune all of his drums. This meant that each drum was individually tuned to a certain note. Most drummers tune their drums so that they are low and often dead sounding, and in the sixties it was hard to pick out what the drummers were doing. Keith didn't like that so he tuned his drums so that they were very open and very ringy, and he did this because he wanted his drums to be heard. He did it on purpose because he wanted to be heard as the lead drummer. He wanted to stand out above everyone else.

"Keith's snare drums were also tuned quite high. This meant they had more of a snap to them. Often his use of the hi-hats was very minimal, especially while performing rather than in the studio. But certainly between 1966 and 1972 he seldom used a hi-hat when he was on the road. This meant there was a constant wash of cymbals, which filled out the overall sound. This mixed with John's bass playing and Pete's powerful distorted guitars and Roger's amazing raspy singing gave The Who their sound and above it all Keith's drumming could still be heard.

"A lot of people see Keith as being a nutcase who just thrashed about on the drums. But he was a brilliant drummer and a very, very clever drummer. He was able to split his body five ways around the drum kit and think ahead and see what could be played before it happened.

"Keith would love to hold down a fairly simple drum beat in the chorus but then in the verse, really open the drums up. This is opposite to how most drummers play. He would really accent some of the notes being played by the other instruments and a lot of drummers don't do that either. Keith was always pushing the boundaries.

"Over the years I have built my drum kit so that it's exactly like Keith's. I use the same size drums and the same Paiste cymbals. Keith was endorsed by Premier drums from 1965 up until the day he died. Keith liked all his drums to be large. He asked Premier for the largest tom that they had and they were 14" by 8", the floor toms were 16" by 18" and the bass drums were 22". Then he just kept adding more and more drums and then a massive gong."

Keith, surrounded by adoring fans, keeps an eye out for the photographer.

DAN MAIDEN-WOOD

ANNA CALVI / DANNY'S LAST CHANCE

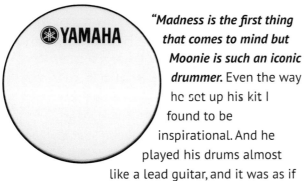

"Madness is the first thing that comes to mind but Moonie is such an iconic drummer. Even the way he set up his kit I found to be inspirational. And he played his drums almost like a lead guitar, and it was as if he refused to play a standard beat. He rarely kept to a standard 4/4, his rolls around the kit were often very intricate and it was exciting. The way Moonie played the drums was very original and because of this he influenced and inspired a lot of people, and some of these people included the greats like Bonham and Baker.

"Moonie changed the way people were allowed to play drums. And he didn't just do this in his style of drumming; he also did it in the way he set up his kit. He would change the set-up all the time. One time he would use a hi-hat, then he would have no hats and instead play everything on the cymbal, then he would move the hi-hats to the right and insert them between the high toms and the floor toms. Keith Moon wasn't afraid to be different and approach things from different angles.

"There was something great about the way that Moonie didn't give a damn and just went out and played the way he wanted to. A lot of drummers can learn from that. It won't work for all drummers but for Moonie it did. The thing is, he didn't mind being out of his comfort zone, but most drummers would struggle with that. Keith Moon really was one of a kind and literally a bit Moonie.

"I started to learn to play the drums when I was about 14. I listened to a lot of early Who stuff because I was into bands like The Jam and other Mod bands of that period. But when I listened to Moonie's drumming I just couldn't get it at all. I tried to emulate what I was hearing but it just blew my mind. His style of drumming is really hard to get your head around.

"The Who wouldn't have been The Who with a different drummer. Simply, they would have been a different band all together. Moonie was one of the musicians in The Who and he played lead solo drums – no one else could have done that."

Left: Keith at Shepperton Studios, 26 May 1978, during the photo shoot with Terry O'Neill for the cover of Who Are You.

MATHEW PRIEST

DODGY

"Keith Moon – the greatest drummer in the world! Moon was a complete force of nature. He is one of the greats and no one will ever be like him, there was no one like him before him and there's no one like him since. He truly was a one-off.

"People like Keith Moon and John Bonham were the pioneers of rock. There just weren't any rock drummers before them. Because there was no rock music, the type of music that Moon listened to was Motown and R&B and jazz. It was the drummers from those bands that Moon had to listen to, they were his contempories. So you had a situation where someone like Keith Moon would be watching Mitch Mitchell and Ringo Starr and they would be doing the same.

"There are many people in recent decades who think they can play like Moon but they grew up with rock and didn't grow up with the music that Moon had and learned from so they will have to

"Even if Moonie hadn't had done all the 'rock'n'roll' stuff, and you took away the drink and drugs and hotels and motor cars, he would still be the greatest rock'n'roll drummer ever."

sound different. Moon got his swing from the tunes he loved and grew up with.

"Moon gave that certain something to The Who that made them sound that way and they swing like a pair of rhino's bollocks. I first heard Keith Moon's drumming when I was nine years old and he made me want to play drums. And all these years later when I hear Moon's drumming I still get a visceral feeling. Whenever I see or hear Keith play it's like I get a shot in the arm. Bang... it's instant!

"My older brother was into bands like The Jam and I listened to his records, The Who was among them and then *Quadrophenia* came along and we watched the film hundreds of times, learning every line in the film... 'Chalky, Chalky the ponce.' There was also a time when Channel 4 used to show episodes of *Ready Steady Go!* before *The Tube* came on, and there would be The Who performing and you just didn't get to see as much footage of Keith playing drums back then.

"I remember seeing a Lou Reed interview from 1966 and the interviewer says: 'So Lou, your music is quite unique. Who do you cite as your influences?' Lou replies: 'Aretha Franklin and The Who.' And that coming from Lou Reed of the Velvet Underground is quite something.

"I heard a story that during some Who recordings Pete Townshend kept asking Moonie to stop playing the 'bloody toms in a certain part', but Moonie couldn't stop himself, so while he was recording a take Townshend was removing parts of Moonie's kit just to prevent him from hitting them. It was the only way they could stop him.

"There are plenty of stories about Keith's wilder side, like smashing up motors and all that, and it's part of it, but only part. I once had a conversation with Daltrey at an after-party following a blue plaque being unveiled for Jimi Hendrix. I was introduced to Daltrey and he begins, 'Oh yeah, you're the drummer from Dodgy who they say sounds like Moonie. Yeah, but what you don't understand is that Moonie was a bastard. Can you imagine what it was like for us being around him for 24 hours a day?' And I sort of understood what he meant. I mean who would want someone knocking on your door at four in the morning waving a bottle of champagne at you? And I get that if people focus too much on that stuff they miss a whole load of other stuff relating to what Moonie was really about. Even if Moonie hadn't done all the 'rock'n'roll' stuff, and you took away the drink and drugs and hotels and motor cars, he would still be the greatest rock'n'roll drummer ever."

SAM KESTEVEN

LIFE-LONG WHO FAN

"I loved Keith Moon, mainly because he looked like a man possessed when he played. A few years back I wrote a letter to *Rhythm* magazine to kind of defend him against the Bonham nuts.

My focus was one song in particular: 'Join Together'. I used to watch the video loads in my teens and practice along; it's a beautiful bit of drumming. There's not a single tom-tom on it. It's a really clever swung pattern with some truly inspired fills… very unlike his trademark chaos. It really showed how versatile he was when he was on form. That letter did get printed too."

Left: Keith discusses the day's festivities with 'Legs' Larry Smith at the Garden Party, which he compered at the Crystal Palace Bowl on 3 June 1972, starring the Beach Boys, Sha Na Na, Joe Cocker, Melanie and Richie Havens. Above: Keith's arrival at the Crystal Palace.

CHRIS PUNTER

COLORYDE

"Sadly I was too young to have met him but my impressions from film and news reports were that of a crazy, hedonistic musician who lived life on the edge.

"I never saw him in the flesh but have viewed and heard much footage of him, both film and heard isolated drum tracks, and on these tracks you can hear Keith screaming while playing and onscreen you see his raw passion and energy with every beat. This is a showman behind the drums, even larger than Roger, the front man.

"My favourite album is *Quadrophenia*. I can play that record over and over. Moonie creates waves, rain, trains and improvises so well on it. All his fills are superb. I also love 'Won't Get Fooled Again', which is one of the tracks I've listened to with isolated drums; it's just pure energy, full of cymbals, accents, crashes, fills. It is complete schizophrenic drumming.

"How would I describe Moon's drumming? Schizophrenic, full of energy, excitement, manic and colourful. In fact I believe he did say when he plays drums he feels he is painting, adding colour, and that is it spot on! Pure showmanship to be honest;

Above: Schizophrenic, full of energy, excitement, manic and colourful! University of Reading, 2 October 1971.

you either watched Pete or Moonie. Most watched Keith because you never knew what was coming. Keith was a very flamboyant, busy, exciting, exploding drummer.

"Inspiration… I would say, for instance Clem Burke of Blondie was so inspired by Moon that he liked to do very clever fills and be a showman, twirling sticks. Every drummer is inspired by Moonie… if they're not then they have no passion. Every drummer I know would love to be Keith! Drummers realised they did not have to be the man sitting at the back holding the beat. They could be… the star of the show. Holding the beat, giving it flare colour and zest… Dave Grohl, Mitch Mitchell, Clem Burke, Reni [Alan Wren], John Bonham. Although some would deny it, they all watched and learned so much from his stage presence because before Moonie, there wasn't any. They learned the art of the entertainer, like Matt Destruction from The Hives is a pure showman inspired by Keith. Keith has inspired me and I must admit sometimes in my bands The Myndset and especially Coloryde I might be a little too busy on the drum fills and crash cymbals.

"I'd say he has left a fantastic backlog of recordings which will inspire and already inspired so many musicians, and not just drummers. People see him and look up to a complete entertainer on and off the stage because he showed so much in his personality. The legacy of Moon is reflected in the wild and wacky tee-shirts. He inspired a generation. His hedonism reflected the moment and time when teenagers did not want to be a mirror image of their parents but individuals, and not living by the polite and expected manners of the time. Moon was not just a rock'n'roll icon but also a reflection of the changing times; times where young people were not satisfied by sensible behaviour and a clean-cut attitude. Moon represented the drug and rule breaking wave that was growing in the disaffected youth of Britain. Music became not just about clean-cut, uniformed band members in matching suits and haircuts, and Moon helped inspire individual and charismatic characters we recognise in bands that followed. He broke the mould of insignificant drummers who previously would have been wallpaper and in the background.

"I'm gutted that he died in such circumstances (trying to stay off the booze and rebuild himself) and far too young, but living to extremes has its price and extreme personalities often burn themselves out. Keith Moon was a complete nutcase who chose to live life to the full, inspiring all drummers not to sit hidden in the background. He was a mind of madness and hedonism, which inspired a generation, and he has left a legacy in his wake."

DIRECT FROM ENGLAND!
HERMAN'S HERMITS

WITH SPECIAL GUESTS

STARS of Monterey Pop Festival
THE WHO "HAPPY JACK"

EXTRA ADDED
First Psychedelic Rock Group in U.S.
THE BLUES MAGOOS

FRIDAY, AUGUST 25th, 6:30 & 9:00 P. M.

KIEL OPERA HOUSE

Tickets $3.00 - $4.00 - $5.00

On Sale At Kiel Auditorium Box Office

Mail Orders To: Hermit's Box Office, Kiel Aud., 1400 Market St.

Enclose Self-Addressed, Stamped Envelope

JOE GIORGIANNI
LIFE-LONG WHO FAN

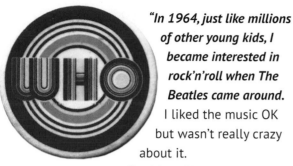

"In 1964, just like millions of other young kids, I became interested in rock'n'roll when The Beatles came around. I liked the music OK but wasn't really crazy about it.

"And, just like a million other young boys, I joined a band sometime in 1966 as a bass player. I was not very good but it gave me a chance to get together with a bunch of other guys and play and talk about music. One day in early 1967 we were having practice at the drummer's house and the radio was playing and 'Happy Jack' came on. There was something about the song that immediately struck me, especially the drums. I had never heard anything quite like it. In late August that summer I was staying with my family at our summer home on Lake Sunnyside in Upstate New York when the singer of our band, Mike Ingalsbe, called asking if I wanted to go to a concert with him in Rochester, New York. The line-up was The Blues Magoos, The Who and Herman's Hermits. I was familiar with The Blues Magoos because of their hit 'Ain't Got Nothing Yet' and we had bought their album. As far as The Who went, of course I still remembered 'Happy Jack' and I had heard something about them smashing their equipment, which somehow intrigued me.

"Mike's mother drove us out to the concert, which was a much, much longer drive than we had thought. It was so long that we had to stay overnight at a motel the night of the show. When we went to the concert at the War Memorial

Auditorium The Blues Magoos opened. I thought I remembered that one of the band members had on a jacket with flashing light panels. In later years I discovered that there were just small blinking lights on the jacket and that Pete Townshend sometimes wore it.

"As they were setting up for The Who a roadie came out and started nailing down the bass drums. Whoa! I also remember them bringing out a basket of drum sticks. Before the show started I believe Keith Moon was running around the stage, wearing a cape like Batman – the TV show was very popular at the time.

"When The Who came on amid much girl screaming (which was also a big thing at the time), there were some things that struck me. The first was that they were using large Fender amplifiers. Also, John Entwistle was playing a white Fender bass with what seemed like a mirror finish pick guard. Also, my eyes weren't very good at the time (I needed glasses) but I was almost positive Pete Townshend was playing a guitar with two necks, which of course he was. When they played 'My Generation' I commented to my buddy standing next to me that it was a song by Count Five. He just looked at me funny. I didn't know at the time that their version on the *Psychotic Reaction* album was a cover of Pete Townshend's song. The Who smashed their equipment at the end among smoke bombs and much mayhem. I remember liking Herman's Hermits but from then on my life had changed. There was really no other band for me but The Who and in the almost 50 years since, that has never changed. To me they are far and away the greatest rock'n'roll band ever. They have the most exciting

Left: A press ad for the show in St Louis, Missouri, on 25 August 1967. Joe Giorgianni went to the Rochester, New York, show on 30 August.

stage act ever and of course a bass player and drummer that have never been equalled.

"A month or two later it was a Sunday night and my brothers and I were watching *The Smothers Brothers Comedy Hour*. I can't remember what band we were expecting to see but when they said it was going to be The Who I told my brothers they were going to see something great. And of course it was.

"I soon bought my first Who album, *Happy Jack*, which happened to be the less common mono pressing. Two things struck me right away – the sound of the guitar, which just seemed to fill every song, and the sound of the drums, which was like nothing else. They just seemed to overpower every song and it felt like the rest of the band was just trying to keep up with the drums. And was any drummer anywhere as fast as Keith Moon was on 'Cobwebs and Strange'?

At around the same time I bought the 'I Can See For Miles' single. Again, the drums just overpowered everything – I was blown away.

"My second album was *The Who Sell Out*. 'Rael' continues to be my number one Who song of all time. Several years ago my young daughter and I were sitting in the car listening to music. I put on 'Rael' and said to her, 'This is what rock'n'roll drumming is all about.' The drums rolls at the end of the song are just unbelievable. Still, the song lacked something – it just seemed unfinished. My thought was proven out when the *Tommy* album came out, as songs like 'Sparks' seemed to pick up where 'Rael' left off. When *Tommy* came out my brothers and I bought it and listened to it. It certainly seemed very different and again the drumming was just exceptional.

"I saw The Who again on 2 August 1971 at the Saratoga Performing Arts Center in Upstate New York on the *Who's Next* tour. By then they were famous and set an attendance record for the venue. I was very nervous about the concert. It just seemed that with The Who anything could happen. That was proven when someone jumped on stage and Pete went over and kicked him as the roadies dragged him off the stage. The couple next to me said they had seen enough and left. By then, though, I realised that a lot of their act was all in fun, with of course Keith leading the festivities.

"My next show was at the Montreal Forum in December 1973 on the *Quadrophenia* tour. I will never forget when the lights went down. In the dark all you could hear was the sound of Keith as he warmed up – it sounded like thunder. When the lights came up it was just like the start of a race. The Who were off and all trying to outdo each other. Those shows went fast. Listening to the *Quadrophenia* album a few weeks ago in 5.1 I was really reminded of how great a drummer Keith was. As good as the writing and performance of the album was, it was Keith who made that album (and all the others) unique.

"The last time I saw The Who with Keith was in December 1975 at the Springfield Civic Center, Massachusetts. The Who were clicking on all cylinders on that tour and it remains for me the greatest rock'n'roll show I have ever seen. I spent a lot of the time at that show watching Keith play but it was hard to take my eyes off of Pete. I commented often after that that if Jesus Christ was onstage you still had to watch Pete.

"In 1978, I learned about Keith's death from the newspaper the morning after he died. I realised then that The Who were now changed forever and would never be the same. I called my friend and fellow Who fan in Boston, who I had met the previous year. There was not really anybody else that would understand the loss. We still remain great friends to this day and still talk every Saturday morning.

"Looking back on the life of Keith I feel a great sadness that he couldn't have lived to be an old rocker like so many others. I suppose the demons and personality that made him great were what gave him such a short life. He still is to me by far the greatest drummer that ever lived."

Keith and Pete on the 1967 US tour, when they toured with Herman's Hermits and The Blues Magoos.

MISS JOSH EMMETT

LIFE-LONG WHO FAN

"The first time I met Keith Moon, whom I called Keefy, was on 13 June 1967 at Detroit Metro Airport. Nancy Lewis sent me a postcard asking me to meet the band until their ride came. I brought them a set of The Hobbit and The Lord of the Rings trilogy. When I gave Keefy his, he signed it and handed it back. I said, 'Noooo. That's for you.' He smiled, 'Thank you, now I'll know it's mine!'

"One night at the Grande Ballroom in Detroit, it was steamy. The only relief was the little fan in the dressing room. The Who finished their first set and the ballroom was cleared. When the second crowd was let in and Pink Floyd was playing, there was a problem with the fan. Keefy said he could fix it. Everyone rolled their eyes. He played around with it for a minute and then I caught his eye. I had noticed that it was unplugged! I tilted my head toward the wall. Keefy reached over and plugged it in and announced, 'See? I fixed it!' When it was time to go on, everyone left the dressing room. When Keefy and I went out, we turned around and went straight back in. It was 120F! We just stood there until the last had left. We looked at the fan and, without a word, we unplugged it and carried it out, down the side, through the little side room and up on the stage. After plugging it in, he sat on his stool and I sat on the floor. Finally, a roadie came up and asked what I was doing. Keefy handed me his drum sticks and I smiled, 'I'm handing Keefy his sticks.' The roadie said, 'I usually do that.' Keefy smiled, 'But

Josh does it better.' When the band was announced and everyone else came on, I switched on the fan. Just before the infamous 'wreck the drum kit', I switched off the fan, unplugged it and moved to the side of the stage. As the band left, Keefy joined me on the floor. We stayed there and dried ourselves off with some towels the roadie threw at Keefy. The place had pretty much emptied out, when we decided to head for the dressing room. When we opened the door, everyone was standing there glaring at us. We turned and walked out. We stood with our backs against the double doors. Then we both said, 'FAN!' We strolled back across

the floor and no one really spoke to us for a while when we came back with it.

"I thought the pictures of Keefy, Kim and Mandy were cute in *Rave* magazine. I got Mandy a Snoopy dog, as Keefy was a big fan, and wrapped it in a

Left and above (and overleaf): All photos by Miss Josh Emmett, taken in Detroit on The Who's US tours of 1967, 1968 and 1970.

shoebox with Peanuts paper. Keefy said that if I didn't tell him what was in the box, he would open it. After I told him, he said he might 'open it anyway!' Next tour I asked if Mandy got her Snoopy and Keefy said, 'Yes! It's on the shelf in her room.'

"My friend Donna and I had a surprise party for Keefy in his room (key supplied by Pete). It looked like a clothes store had exploded. We folded and hung and put away. Later, Keefy said, 'That might be the best present I got! I can pack tomorrow all by myself!' When Keefy came in, followed by the band (except Roger), some roadies and a manager with his groupie, and turned on the light, we yelled, 'SURPRISE!' Later I asked him if he really was

and wrote the captions I made up. In one group, I had Keefy telling a story about a bunny who came to a bad end. There was one shot I liked where you can see him playing drums and Roger's trousers framing the picture. Caption: 'Keith between Roger's legs.' It was voted the best for reasons other than what I meant, thank you John. I asked Keefy what he thought of the scrapbook and he looked at me seriously with those big eyes, 'I love it! But I would never do something like that for you.' He gave me a big hug. I knew what Keefy meant. We had ADHD and I had to have Donna actually do it. Finally, the manager said they had to get to the 'real' party and they trooped across the hall to a room they had

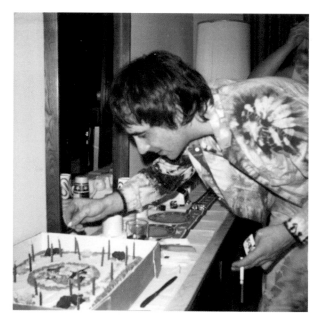 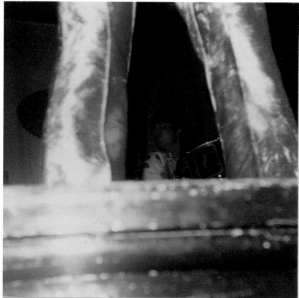

surprised and he said, 'If I had been any more surprised, we would have had to have had the party in the hospital.' And he touched his heart. But, apparently, we would have still had the party. After he blew out the candles, he relit them over and over so everyone could have a wish too. At first he kept lighting matches until, finally, he just lit a plastic fork because it would last longer. We gave him a scrapbook we made of my pictures. I picked out ones I really liked and Donna taped them in

rented. We cleaned up Keefy's room and went over. It was packed wall-to-wall. I had Keefy's key. He was standing on one of the beds putting a rifle together. He waved at me. I was about 90 lbs, so I went in. I got between the beds and Keefy pulled me up. He thanked me again for the wonderful party and gave me another big hug. He put me back on the floor and picked up the rifle parts. I dropped to my knees and crawled out (a trick I learned from Rod Stewart)."

LORENA PEREIRA

LIFE-LONG WHO FAN

"I'm Lorena, and I'm only 18. I've known The Who for a long time, but only about two years ago they got really important to me. And it has a lot to do with Keith. I have social anxiety, so it's always been really hard for me to socialise and sometimes I get really sad and nervous about nothing really. So, two years ago, I was watching *The Rolling Stones Rock'n'Roll Circus* for the first time and when The Who appeared playing 'A Quick One', I just couldn't think about anything else! I kept looking at that crazy, shining, brilliant drummer, who'd sing all the words and shake his head, scream, throw part of his drum kit over his own head... I just felt so happy just to look at him perform. I can't even explain it in words.

"So I searched all about this young man, who had made me happier in 10 minutes than I'd ever been. And I started to read all about how crazy he was, throwing his car into swimming pools, destroying hotel rooms and all, and that was all pretty nice but I was actually looking for how he was as a human being (well, that's something I usually do). I started to feel so frustrated that people only talked about him as 'Moon The Loon' when I knew he could be more than that, he could be this amazing loving person (that I have never had a chance to meet). I watched every single documentary about The Who, every piece of footage I could find, every interview. I've read books, old magazines, and more important than anything, I've listened to their songs. Always looking for a way to

'meet' the Keith Moon I love.

"All of this journey to find a way to connect with Moon made me a lot more of a happy person, a lot more confident than I ever was. Every time I felt bad about myself I knew I could just put some Who record on and I'd start to feel incredible! Every time I felt shy and scared, I could just think about how amazing Keith was and how he could do every single thing he wanted to and I'd not be afraid to do what I wanted to. And this still works for me. If I've made amazing stuff in my life, that I'd NEVER do before, in these last two years, it's all because of Keith and The Who. They gave me the power to be whoever I wanted to be.

"I keep making up ways to be closer to Keith, I once said that he must have been something in my past life, like someone really important to me, because I actually feel we've already met (and believe me, I was never a religious person!) and I miss him. And when the moon is full and bright in the sky, I can feel he's up there, looking at me and at every single one of his fans.

"I may be too young, and people may say it's all very foolish that I feel that way, but they don't even know how good it is to me to put on the Isle of Wight '70 gig and watch Keith Moon playing the drums so happily and so naturally that it makes me feel happy too.

"He's my angel. He always saves me from all the boredom, sadness and anxiety that surround me. He was unique. The one and only Keith Moon, who amazed me with his talent, his drumming, his madness, his sweet eyes, and more than anything, his passion for being who he was and making people feel happy."

Right: The Who perform 'A Quick One (While He's Away)' on the set of The Rolling Stones Rock'n'Roll Circus, 11 December 1968.

HARRISON KRAMER

LIFE-LONG WHO FAN

"Keith Moon is a huge inspiration for me. I am 14-years old and have severe OCD and depression. I even missed nearly a whole year of school because of my anxiety disorder.

"I found music to be my therapy, especially that of The Who. I love drumming, and I am always intrigued by those who perform. The way the beat flows and the capabilities of certain drummers really make a song what it is.

"Keith Moon not only is a master of the instrument, but learning how he turned his anxieties into art really inspires me to keep pushing forward and trying new things. Because of Keith, I learned to turn my depression into art and pursue whatever endeavour that interests me, and to keep pushing forward to the greatest limit to achieve my goal. Therefore, that is how Keith Moon's legacy made an impact on my life."

An inspiration to so many, even now nearly 40 years after his death.

JONATHAN LOUIS

DRUMMER AND LIFE-LONG WHO FAN

"I was 10 years old, and I didn't really like any music at all until my dad and I were driving down the highway and he put a Who's greatest hits album into the CD player.

He skipped ahead to track eight, I believe, and at first, Pete Townshend's looped keyboard intro bored the hell out of me, but when the band came in around the 30-second mark, I was introduced to 'Won't Get Fooled Again', and to rock'n'roll. However, it was the orchestral and monumental power of the madman Keith Moon that stood out to me the most,

especially because Moon's drum solo was the first drum solo I ever heard. I had no idea the drums could be that powerful and upfront. However, it wasn't until I played 'Won't Get Fooled Again' on the video game *Rock Band* that I truly appreciated it and was blown away at how unorthodox Moon's drumming was. It was one of three songs I couldn't play on Expert. I then asked my parents for a drum set for Christmas and began taking lessons, and have been playing real drums for six years. I have so much fun playing drums and have been in several bands. I'm 18 years old now and playing in a successful rock'n'roll band is what I want to do with my life, all because of the legendary wild man himself, Mr Keith John Moon."

The Who on their 1973 Quadrophenia tour.

JOE GORELICK

DRUMMER AND LIFE-LONG WHO FAN

"*I was just 10 years old when Keith Moon left this earth, but his style, his recordings, the live videos all made me the drummer I am today.*

If you only listen to his playing on *Live At Leeds*, you'd hear the absolute genius of his thinking, the sheer force of musicality in his playing, his loving relationship to the other three band members, and the sense of humour that came through on every bar. His sense of whimsy was coming through on even angrier tracks like 'Won't Get Fooled Again' where the intro alone was unique to any drummer's perception of where the door to enter the song would, or should, be. He was a one of a kind human, a one of a kind drummer and never to be forgotten or replaced. We owe him a lot of respect and I owe my drums to him. I miss him."

Keith's last farewell, Shepperton Studios, 25 May 1978, during filming for The Kids Are Alright *movie.*

The Who in January 1966, in London's West End for a publicity photo shoot, with Keith sporting his 'Elvis For Everyone' badge.

NATHAN HERSHFELD

LIFE-LONG WHO FAN

"I am now 54 years old. I have been a life-long Who fan since I first heard a copy of **The Who Sell Out** *while tripping in 1974.* I first saw The Who at the 1976 Anaheim Stadium show. I still have the tee-shirt and ticket stub for $10. I have seen them many times since.

Just about every North American tour.

"Back when Keith's *Two Sides Of The Moon* album was either out or coming out, he did a live radio call-in in Los Angeles. I was able to get through and talk to him. I was really young and nervous, but I asked him, 'What instrument do you use when you write your own songs?' From the other end of the phone came his maniacal laugh and then he shouted 'a pen and a flat'. I will never forget that as long as I live. He was the greatest."

Keith and Annette Walter-Lax on the cover of Keith's solo album Two Sides Of The Moon.

GEORGE MANNEY

LIFE-LONG WHO FAN

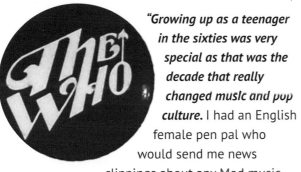

"Growing up as a teenager in the sixties was very special as that was the decade that really changed music and pop culture. I had an English female pen pal who would send me news clippings about any Mod music, clothes or newsworthy articles, as in America we only had a small group of individuals and magazines who reported this fashion and music movement in the UK.

"When I first heard 'My Generation' I was hooked! Then when I saw their clothes and Pop Art direction it all made sense to me, plus they covered James Brown on their first LP. Moon and The Who were Mod rebellion and that spoke to me in volumes.

"Moon's drumming was so captivating with his joy and lunacy as it was an extension of his inner child. All kids love to bang a drum! And that was me too.

"When you saw the band in concert, it was as if there were three leaders all competing for attention... Moon, Roger and Pete. But it was Moon's drumming that created that sense of crime... standing on his kit, smashing everything in sight and kicking the kit over into the crowd.

"I got to meet Keith backstage for the first time at JFK Stadium in Philadelphia. Pink Floyd was on the bill and played but The Who did not, due to heavy rain. My friend and I made it back to their dressing room and Roger and Pete were fighting over something. Then all of a sudden Keith comes thrashing in with a young girl in tow. Next thing I know, their tour manager grabs us and throws us out of the room. Now I was only 17 and this was just 'madness' and I really wanted to be in a big rock group like them!

"The second time I got to see Keith again was at the Electric Factory for their first performance of *Tommy*, in 1969. Moon was running around backstage in his underwear rolling tobacco and hash. What was interesting about his drum set-up was... he had a second floor tom-tom but that was to hold towels for him and no hi-hat stand! And when he played he became that cheerful and mischievous boy that we all could relate to as teenagers. Keith's drumming was totally free and alive as is noticeable in his cymbal style... hitting them as often as possible and off the beat like jazz drummers do.

"Moon and The Who were my first exposure to a performance art band! Long live rock and Keith Moon!"

SHAWN LACKIE

DRUMMER AND LIFE-LONG WHO FAN

"*I have been a Who fan since 1964 and more specifically a Keith Moon fan.* Being a drummer myself I had a huge appreciation of just what Moonie brought to the band. So to say I was thrilled when I got a pair of tickets for their 1976 show in Toronto would be an understatement. When I bought the tickets the only ones left were what were called 'obstructed view'. I didn't care. I was going to be there and that was all that mattered.

"However, when we got there it was a dream come true, we were up behind the stage and I had a clear and unobstructed view of Keith Moon. As always the show was a ball buster, but things got interesting when they launched into the start of 'Baba O'Riley'. Roger was in full strut that night and Moon's crazy ways kicked in because when the intro to 'Baba O'Riley' started playing Roger was strutting like a peacock.

"Guess Keith wanted to speed things up (and deflate some of Roger's antics) so he threw one of his sticks at Roger and it hit him in the back. Daltrey turned around and the look he shot Moonie would have killed a bull elephant. But Moonie was in high gear and laughing like a hyena.

"The song kicked in and they got back to the biz at hand but it was a moment I will never forget, Moonie's high jinks in full display. It was an awesome show. Sadly that was the last show they would do together."

THE **WHO TOUR**

THE WHO

USA & CANADA

October 6—Phoenix, AZ
October 7—San Diego, CA
October 9 & 10—Oakland, CA
October 13—Portland, OR
October 14—Seattle, WA
October 16—Edmonton, Alberta
October 18—Winnipeg, Manitoba
October 21 & 22—Toronto, Ontario

MCA RECORDS

Left: Keith would dress up at the slightest opportunity–whether it was as a bell boy, a jester, a bear, as Hitler, or even in full drag, and as this gem from The Who's archive shows, a festive Santa Claus.

RENEE KATHLEEN

DRUMMER AND LIFE-LONG WHO FAN

Rock'n'roll and all things drumming had already cast its spell when I was three and living in California. The Beatles and early Who songs were the 45s I loved most of all in my collection. By the time I was 13 and taking piano lessons, I wanted nothing more than to get serious about playing the drums, my first love.

"I owned both versions of the rock opera *Tommy*, the original by The Who and the London Symphony Orchestra's version. By the time the movie came out, along with the soundtrack in 1975, I knew every phrase, chorus and solo of that incredible album.

"I will forever remember the very second I first saw Keith Moon light up the kit and the movie screen! If I had thought drumming had me under its spell, it was nothing compared to the magic Moonie cast. He was all arms, speed and passion. And I was excited, enthralled, thrilled and inspired all at once. I found his portrayal of Uncle Ernie nothing short of mesmerising, and it was both, comic and compelling. I literally lost count of how many times I saw the movie, stopping at around 33.

"I immediately sought every Who album ever pressed, and proceeded to make their music my absolute study, day and night. As this was prior to MTV, rock videos or YouTube, you had to wait and hope for a rock clip, on *Don Kirshner's Rock Concert* or *The Midnight Special*. Talk show host Merv Griffin took a chance to have Moon on his show, and the episode was one of true hysteria and comic chaos.

"By the time I got a used, beat-up drum set, I had every triplet and every fill committed to memory and I was ready! *Live At Leeds* on a quad stereo, and a set of headphones? It was assured that I would have neighbours that absolutely despised me! *Live At Leeds* remains some of the most rough and raw blues rock ever recorded.

"Those days on that ratty kit were the best days of my life, as I attempted to follow Moon's style of power and passion. His drumming was a reflection of his personality – so full of witty, wild and joyous abandon.

"*Quadrophenia* took Keith's drum style to a whole new level. It is nothing short of a masterpiece, where Keith was at the peak of his drumming game. His massive kit was a deliberate symphony of the maturity of his range and his expression. His orchestral and melodic approach to the fills and the phrasing was heartfelt, soulful and commanding. 'The Rock', 'Love Reign O'er Me' and 'Bell Boy' stand out as diamonds among gems and the music still brings the chills. It remains a timeless classic, in every way.

"I was barely 15 when the local station announced they would come to Jacksonville, Florida – a city quite far from my rural home at the time. My mother knew my love of this band, particularly the drummer, and gave her permission for me to take a Greyhound bus, to see them at the Gator Bowl.

"While there was some real trouble at that concert for myself and my friend, it was incredible just to see Keith Moon. It was truly the ultimate moment in the life of a drummer and a rock'n'roller! I was not aware that two days later, Keith would wind up in a Miami psych ward, battling alcoholism and depression, or that it would be one of his last stage performances.

"I went on to play drums in the high school

band, and had just been accepted as a percussionist for the town symphony when I heard the news of his death. I was devastated. I contacted MCA Records and Universal Studios to obtain information, and any further details they could give me. I was given an address in England where I could send my poetry and portraits I painted of him to his mother Kit. I made a solemn vow to play drums for the rest of my life, in his honour.

"When I finally realised my dream to visit England, it was his face I had tattooed on my arm, and it was Curzon Street – the site of his demise – that was my first stop in London. Keith was a force of nature. He was funny and tragic and one of kind. His drumming left a legacy and inspired generations of drummers, and will continue to inspire generations to come."

Keith as wicked Uncle Ernie in the Ken Russell film of Tommy.

JAY MAHONEY

DRUMMER AND LIFE-LONG WHO FAN

"*I have played drums since 1960.* I have a master's in music education with a concentration on percussion. I listened to thousands of drummers in my lifetime, and Keith Moon is one of two that are my primary playing influences.

"He was always part of the melody of The Who. Trying to explain that to my friends and family was challenging, but I ended up having them listen to a Who track through the left side of a pair of headphones so they heard the bass. I'd then 'keep time' for that song that they would hear in the other ear. Then I'd have them listen to the track with the headphones entirely on. Instant Keith Moon and Who fans were created.

"Nothing has ever matched the energy, ferocity and unique melodic influence of Keith. I saw the band in Chicago in 1971 and 17 times since. My kids' first Who concert was in 1999. They understand and love Keith Moon. Talkin' about our generations."

JOE RAMERSA

DRUMMER AND LIFE-LONG WHO FAN

"Being a drummer myself, of course I would have my influences; Mr Moon was right up there on a very short list of what I consider the best. He was a feast for the ears and the eyes. He breaks all the rules in today's popular drumming style and in my mind the only band he could have ever played in was The Who.

"Keith Moon was the Bruce Lee or the Evel Knievel of the drums, a train going 100 miles per hour around a hairpin corner on a cliff best describes his playing. I can't imagine my life without Keith Moon."

In October 1972, The Who sponsored a car in the Daily Mail Rally of Great Britain. At the press party Keith arrived, for no particular reason, dressed as a bear–or is that a giant rat? Here Pete tries the head on for size.

MICHAEL BUTLER

LIFE-LONG WHO FAN

"It was the mid-seventies, I was a teenager and I was fortunate to win a lottery to get Who tickets at Madison Square Garden in New York. My friend and I had great seats on the left side of the stage, about 10 rows up.

Keith was really sick that night. He had a large fan blowing on him and he was wearing a white towel around his neck. I remember the band playing 'Behind Blue Eyes'. Keith was being attended to behind his drum kit. As the drum part was approaching, Keith hopped back on his throne and proceeded to pound the drums, never missing a beat. I will never forget that moment."

Left: One of several shots taken of Keith that were used for US press ads for 'Won't Get Fooled Again' with the caption, 'Who's next?'

Above: Never missing a beat, Keith pounding his enormous drum kit.

SUE GILLIES

DRUMMER AND LIFE-LONG WHO FAN

"My story starts at 15 when I first heard The Who. I had started playing along to records at 14 as I loved the drums and was told I had a good beat. There weren't many female drummers at the time as it was the early eighties.

Quadrophenia was my first record and I played along to every song and then bought every album I could get my hands on. Because of Moon's style, every band I auditioned for I was asked to join.

"Flash forward over 30 years later and I have played with hundreds of musicians in Boston and NYC including Mick Taylor of The Rolling Stones, Elliott Randall of Steely Dan and The Holmes Brothers. Keith Moon was my main influence when I started when I was a teenager and I can't thank him enough."

JANE QUINN

LIFE-LONG WHO FAN

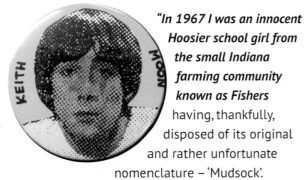

"In 1967 I was an innocent Hoosier school girl from the small Indiana farming community known as Fishers having, thankfully, disposed of its original and rather unfortunate nomenclature – 'Mudsock'.

In 1967 Keith Moon was a highly successful rock'n'roll drummer from the swinging town of London, England. He'd just turned 21 and was touring the USA in a modified yellow school bus. He was cool. I was not. Our paths were destined to cross more than once.

"This is the story of my original close encounter (of the third kind) with Moonie. The meeting took place where most such meetings take place: the tour bus outside the venue. He was inside. I was outside. We shared a 'moment' as our eyes met. Well, maybe it was more like a second, but shared nonetheless. Then Keith Moon leaned out of the bus window and sang to me. It was not, however, a Who song. It was, in fact, the newest Beatle song, 'Hello, Goodbye'. Yes, in 1967 everyone in the world, including Moonie, was obsessed with The Beatles.

Following my personal serenade, he handed me his Coca-Cola bottle along with a small bit of the abused drum skin from the evening's concert. I went away a happy camper. The bottle found a loving home in my teenage bedroom where a makeshift shrine grew around it. Friends and acquaintances made the pilgrimage to Fishers, Indiana, to visit the Shrine of the Moon. Although we knew nothing of such futuristic things as cloning, we lived in hope that Moonie might somehow physically manifest from the glass bottle as if a genie escaping from a lamp.

"The story has an abrupt and sad ending. One day I arrived home from school to find the shrine empty. As this was back in the day of glass bottles and deposits on glass bottles and reuse of glass bottles, my mother decided it worthy to deliver the famous Keith Moon Coca-Cola bottle to the local supermarket where she swapped it for the original two cent deposit. I don't think I ever fully forgave her."

Keith's come a long, long way with Premier...maybe you could too!

There can't be more than a few drummers who could afford an outfit like Keith's. It's probably the world's most expensive set of drums.

But whatever the price, it's the SOUND that counts with Premier. Because *all* Premier drums are made to the same very high standards.

Whether you're a big star like Keith, or hopefully setting out on the long climb up, you'll get the best sounds from Premier.

You'll get the best service too . . .

PICTURE CREDITS *Every effort has been made to trace the copyright holders of the photographs in this book but one or two were unreachable. We would be grateful if the photographers concerned would contact us.* **Getty Images** *Front endpaper The Visualeyes Archive, 4 Mickey Adair, 9 Rhythm Magazine, 10 Terry O'Neill, 11btm Chris Morphet, 12 K & K Ulf Kruger OHG, 14 Jan Olofsson, 23 Chris Morphet, 24 David Warner Ellis, 39 Leni Sinclair, 77 Jim Barron, 106 2Michael Ochs Archives, 114 Anwar Hussein, 121 Paul Ryan, 122 Mickey Adair, 123 RB, 124 Jack Kay, 127 Michael Putland, 132 Michael Ochs Archives, 135 Anwar Hussein, 177 Philippe le Tellier, 183 Michael Ochs Archives. Back endpaper Jack Kay.* **Rex Features** *20 Richard Young/Rex/Shutterstock.* **Richard Evans** *6, 43, 52t, 74, 115.* **Trinifold Archive** *2, 8, 11t Terry O'Neill, 13, 17 Terry O'Neill, 18/19 Aubrey Dewar, 25, 26, 27, 28, 32/33 Aubrey Dewar, 36, 41, 42, 46, 49, 51, 53, 56, 57, 59 both, 60, 71 David Wedgbury, 72, 76, 80, 82, 85, 86, 88, 91, 92, 95, 96, 99 Chris Morphet, 100, 103, 104/5, 106, 111, 112, 116/117 Hipgnosis, 118, 130, 134, 136, 138, 140, 142 Kevin Stein, 144, 145, 147, 148, 152 Vincent McEvoy, 155, 156 Terry O'Neill, 158, 160, 161, 164, 167, 173, 174, 175, 176 Kevin Stein, 180, 184, 185, 186, 187, 188 Aubrey Dewar, 189 Tom Wright, 190 Premier Drum Company.* **Alamy** *37 © Trinity Mirror / Mirrorpix / Alamy Stock Photo.* **Mirrorpix** *44 Ron Burton, 55 Tom King, 152 Mirrorpix.* **Peter Butler** *52 bl, 52 br, 54 bl, 54 br, 64.* **Barrie Wentzell** *62, Courtesy of the Moon Family 65, 151.* **Courtesy of John Schollar and The Beachcombers** *66, 67, 68.* **Bob Gruen** *75.* **Brad Rogers** *128, 129.* **Kaitlin Hawk** *146.* **Jeff Ragland / The Pearl Drum Company** *149.* **MCA Records** *150, 178.* **Miss Josh Emmett** *168, 169, 170, 171.*

KEITH MOON *BRITISH PATENT EXPLODING DRUMMER*

Keith's most famous drum kit was the Pictures of Lily kit that was built for Keith by Premier Drums, with whom he had signed an exclusive endorsement deal on 6 September 1965, using his specifications and suggestions for the design. It featured images of 'Lily' – a sort of twenties-style stripper, photographed from the rear, 'The Who' written in yellow perspective type on a pink background and 'Keith Moon Patent British Exploding Drummer' written in pink against a black background. He first used the kit on 7 July 1967 at the Malibu Beach and Shore Club on Lido Beach in New York. It's believed that at least four such kits were manufactured for Keith's use.

Although Premier Drums built the kit, using birch wood, they did include parts from Gretsch and Rogers drums. The kit comprised two 22" x 14" bass drums, three 16" floor toms (two 16" x 18" and one 16" x 16"), three 14" x 8" mounted toms and a 14" x 5½" snare drum. Additionally Keith used Premier Lok-fast cymbal stands and a Premier bass drum pedal (250). In 2006 Premier Drums produced a replica of the original kit, calling it the Spirit Of Lily Limited Edition. The first kit made was auctioned off and the money donated by Premier to the Teenage Cancer Trust.

Nowadays parts of the original Pictures of Lily kit can be found in various places around the globe. There are some in Brad Roger's collection, some at the Rock'n'roll Hall of Fame in Cleveland, Ohio, and some in the Victoria & Albert Museum in London.

And the whereabouts of some parts are unknown.

Keith talking to *Beat Instrumental* in 1967: "At first I wondered what to talk about, but then I realised that the obvious subject was my new drum kit. I don't have it at the moment; it's down at the Bristol Siddeley factory having its engines fitted. No, I'm serious. This kit has to be seen to be believed. It's going to be called 'The Keith Moon Patent British Exploding Drum Kit'. I'm having the shells strengthened and made more resonant but the drums will still be basically Premier.

"The drums are covered in gaudy designs painted in Dayglo and on stage they'll light up larger than life. I'd like to say a bit more about the engine and what it will do but I think I'd prefer you to see the kit in action. I can promise you that it will be really worth seeing. It will give this effect of exploding, hence the name. I'm not sure what the situation is regarding copies of the new kit, but I dare say there will be a version for sale, although I can't see everyone wanting Keith Moon designs."

Keith did, of course, use other drum kits during his playing years, and how many he destroyed is unknown, but it was a lot. As the years rolled by Keith tried all sorts of arrangements and amounts of drums and cymbals. He even gave one of his kits to Ringo Starr, who in turn gave it to his son Zak, who in turn gave it to Sotheby's to sell in 1992. Keith originally wanted the fittings on this cream/white Premier kit to be gold-plated but Premier managed to talk Keith out of this idea and to settle for copper instead. During the mid-seventies Keith also preferred to use a Gretsch (14") snare drum rather than a Premier one.

Left: One of Premier's first whole page advertisements from 1967 which included Keith with his Pictures of Lily kit.